D1569339

BREAKING INTO TV NEWS

How To Get A Job & Excel As A TV Reporter-Photographer

MIKE CARROLL
TV News Reporter
Photographer
Video Editor

MIKECARROLLFILMS.COM

MIKECARROLLFILMS.COM

BOOKS BY MIKE CARROLL

NAKED FILMMAKING: How To Make A Feature-Length Film—Without A Crew—For $10,000 Or Less

FILMS BY MIKE CARROLL ON DVD
& DIGITAL DOWNLOAD

Dog Soldiers: The Dogumentary
Year
Nightbeats

The photograph on the previous page of Mike Carroll interviewing Doris Miller was taken by Nancy Siegler at her sunflower garden. Nancy is a breast cancer survivor who annually opens her garden to the public as a fundraiser for the American Cancer Society. (nancysieglerphotography.com).

mikecarrollfilms.com

ISBN-13: 978-1470169152

ISBN-10: 1470169150

First Edition: April 2012

Dedicated to Mike Dieffenbach,
Steve Ramsey and Jim Anderson.

*The roles these men played in my life are detailed in
the early chapters of this book. Without their help,
guidance and willingness to give me a chance I
honestly don't think I'd have had the career with a
camera that I've enjoyed for the past three decades.*

Table of Contents

Glossary

A-roll
The primary audio, natural sound and interview bites in a TV news story.

B-roll
Video that plays while you hear a reporter's or anchor's track telling the story.

Bite
A portion of an interview used in a news story, typically running from four to twelve seconds.

Dynamic Angle
When the camera is in close and very wide on an object or activity that is happening in front of the camera lens. Example: A ground-level wide angle shot of a building, then the wheel of a car rolls into the frame very large in the foreground, literally inches from the camera lens.

E.P.
Executive Producer—This person oversees all the newscasts and reviews and approves all news scripts, checking them for factual and spelling errors, because the script may run simultaneously with the story in Closed Captioning for the hearing impaired. Since many people—reporters, producers and writers—are writing scripts for a newscast, the E.P. makes sure that the style and quality of writing is consistent.

HFR
"Hold For Release"—A story that is not scheduled to be shot and aired the same day. Typically a series or special project piece that is shot days or weeks prior to being broadcast, or a franchise segment, such as a health desk story.

IFB
"Interruptible Feedback"—An earpiece that an anchor or reporter wears during a newscast or live shot that allows a producer to speak to them or give them cues.

Intro
The two to three sentence introduction that an anchor makes when introducing a news story or reporter live shot.

Look-Live
When a reporter records a stand-up intro to their package, and concludes with a stand-up close, giving the appearance of doing a live shot, although the word "live" is never used. In the case of a look-live an anchor would simply intro the story the same as any other package, as opposed to saying, "Now we go live to Mike Carroll. . . ."

Market
The industry term for a city or "coverage area" that a TV station's broadcast signal covers, determined by geography and population—the number of households and potential viewers in that area. The general public may refer to Boston as, "A great city." TV people would call it, "A great market," based on the market size and quality of the news.

Mic
Short for "microphone."

Nat Pack—Natural Sound Package
A package, typically done by a photographer, where the story is told entirely through interviews, video and natural sound.

One-Man Band
A Midwest TV term for a reporter-photographer. A person who does double-duty as both cameraman and reporter, not to mention being their own editor as well. In larger TV markets a "one-man band" most often refers to a photographer who shoots a story as well as running a microwave truck for live shots.

One-Stop Shopping
Where all the shooting for a story is done at one location, such as a blood drive, a job fair, a parade, etc.

Package
A fully-edited TV news story comprising a recorded reporter audio track, interview bites and B-roll. It may end with a reporter stand-up close or just a voice-over tag ("sig out") such as, "In San Francisco, I'm Mike Carroll, KCRA-3 Reports." A package may play inside a reporter's live shot and be "open-ended," meaning that at the end of the package the reporter will appear live again to close the story out.

Real Estate Shots
Industry slang for establishing shots of a building or general shots of an area or location.

Sig Out
Signature Out—When a reporter closes a story by saying, "In San Francisco, I'm Mike Carroll, KCRA-3 Reports."

SOT
Sound On Tape—Another term for an interview bite.

Sticks
News slang for a camera tripod

Tag or Tag Out

Same as a sig out—When a reporter signs off at the end of a story.

VO

Voice Over—When an on-air anchor reads a news script while B-roll video plays on the screen.

VO-SOT

Voice Over-Sound On Tape—Pronounced "V-O-S-O-T," "V-O-Sot" or "Vo-Sot." When an anchor reads a script describing a story for about twenty-to-thirty seconds as video is played, leading to a five-to-fifteen second interview bite, or Sound On Tape. Stories can vary in a newscast and simply be a VO, a VO-SOT, an SOT-VO, or just an SOT.

VO Patrol

When a photographer is given a list of assignments and sent out around the city to shoot stories on his or her own—such as a walk for charity or the ribbon-cutting of a new library or something for the sports department—all to be run as VOs or VO-SOTs on a newscast.

True Confessions

I'm not a full-time reporter-photographer. I only get to do it occasionally. I'd like to do it more often, and I have no doubt that a few years down the road that's going to happen, whether it's by choice or not. I asked to be allowed to shoot and report because I see it as the future of broadcast journalism. It's also survival. I was working in Los Angeles in 1985 when all the stations employed two-man camera crews—one person shot the camera and the other recorded the sound. By 1986 the one-piece Sony BetaCam hit the streets—and so had every broadcast news soundman. I love how technology makes our lives easier, but I've also seen it take away livelihoods. I don't want to be expendable.

I've been a professional TV news cameraman since 1983. I voluntarily jumped into doing photographer-reporting a year later. Then, for a long time, I worked as strictly a photographer, or a photographer-editor. It's only been in the past couple of years, as the industry's been reinventing itself, that I've been able to step back into the reporting shoes again. I don't do it on an every day basis—yet. As you'll find in the interviews with other industry professionals, there are some full-time reporters who only get to do both jobs once or twice a week. There are also interviews with reporter-photographers, or multi-media journalists, who are out on the streets juggling a good many jobs from the moment their workday starts until it's time to head home.

If your ambition is to be a TV news reporter, you've probably put all your emphasis into learning how to write and report, leaving the technical aspects of the business for last—if at all. In that case, this book should help to fill in some of those gaps.

For me, a camera has always been a tool for telling a story. I'm not a big fan of flashy, effects-driven stories. I rarely even use tripods and lights. I believe that simpler is better. But there's no way around it, television is a technical beast. It's about cameras, microphones, cables, lights, computers, and almost anything else that requires an electrical power source. If you want to be in this business, you're going to have to learn what all this is and how to use it. Hopefully, this book can help you sort through it a little better.

This Is *Your* Book

When I pick up a book like this, I tend not to start at the beginning, but go through the table of contents to find the sections that interest me most and inhale those sections first. Eventually I work my way through the rest of it.

If you're the type of person who starts with the title page, goes on to the dedication, the forward, then settles in on page one and goes on from there, that's great because that's the way I set the book up. However, it's not required.

The point I'm trying to make is: Use this book the way that works best for you. If you choose to start at the beginning and find out about my backstory and what my first year in the business was like, thanks and please enjoy. If you'd rather bypass that and jump right into the section on internships and how to get your own career going, go for it. If you're more interested in what you should be doing with a website, start there. If your primary interest is the camera and technical stuff, that's in the table of contents under "Shooting" and "Gear."

I wrote this to provide a little more knowledge on how to navigate a career and a life in TV news. It's what I've experienced, learned, observed, and the methods that work for me. Use what you can, adapt it to your own needs, or find your own way entirely. *It's your book.* And let me know if it helps you in any way.

This Book & My Blog

Portions of this book have appeared in blogs on my website, mikecarrollfilms.com, where I try to post videos of all the stories I do as a reporter-photographer, along with behind-the-scenes info on how they were done. What has been reproduced on these pages has been expanded and significantly revised and edited. None of the scripts or notes exploring the writing process that are in this book have ever been published. What appears on these pages is significantly more complete.

I regularly update the site with information on the latest news stories and other work I'm doing, so it's worth bookmarking the site and checking in from time to time.

Note on Running Times

News stories have limitations on how long they can run. In newspapers it's determined by word count—500 words, 1,000 words and so on. TV news stories are based on time—a minute-fifteen seconds, a minute-and-a-half, two minutes, and so on.

Running times throughout this book will be printed numerically in minutes and seconds, such as 1:15, 1:30, 2:00. When you see 1:35 on a page it means one minute and thirty-five seconds, and not one thirty-five in the afternoon.

This is the way we write the times in the business, so you might as well get used to it now.

Interviews And Photos

Everyone interviewed in this book was extremely generous in talking to me and sharing their stories. Some people I knew before. Others were recommended to me and we've only spoken over the phone. The interviews have been edited for clarity and to arrange their stories in chronological order. Each person interviewed reviewed the edited transcript of their interview to correct, expand or delete and had total approval over their own words.

I had no idea what anyone was going to say and no one was asked to be interviewed because their views would coincide with mine. That most of what everyone says is similar can only be attributed to the fact that we all work in the same business.

Their participation in this book should in no way be regarded as an endorsement of this book any farther than the chapters dealing with their own interviews. Their views and working methods are their own, just as the rest of the book dealing with my own story and working methods are my own.

GETTING A JOB IN TV NEWS

First Rule of TV News: Never Miss A Deadline
The odds against you often seem ridiculous. You're sent out on stories where you're expected to find sources, people to interview, a perfect live shot location—and be on the air in just a few hours.

Yet, most of the time we manage to do it.

You can be the best reporter anybody's seen, but if you take too long and miss more than a couple deadlines, your future in daily news will be short-lived. On the other hand, you could be the world's most mediocre reporter, but as long as you make your deadlines, even if it's only by the skin of your teeth, you're going to be okay.

Digital Opportunity Knocks

I WAS HEADING OUT THE NEWSROOM at the end of the day when Anzio Williams, the news director at KCRA-TV, invited me into his office to talk. Never something you want to have happen on a Friday. The corporate world is notorious for lowering the boom on Fridays. "Am I still going to have a job when I come out of this office?" I wondered. I knew I should have gone out through the back door.

Anzio told me how he'd seen some of the stories I'd done by myself, shooting the interviews and video and cross-cutting them together into natural sound packages, or "nat packs." He'd also noticed that I was frequently sent out on my own to gather the elements for stories, which would then be handed over to a reporter or anchor to write up, giving the appearance that they had gone out to cover that story themselves. (My favorite days are often when I get to work on my own in the field.)

I had no idea where any of this was heading when he said, "So, Mike, what is it you want to do?"

I wasn't sure where this had come from, but the question had been put before me and I decided to take a chance and put out an idea that had been brewing in my head for a while.

"Well, frankly, I'd like to do my own reporting. I'd really like to put out one of these stories that I'm sent out to cover by myself, and write it, track it with my own voice and tag it out with my name on air, just like one of the other reporters."

"You mean like an MMJ or one of these digital journalists."

"Yes. I did it twenty-five years ago when I started out in the business and I liked it. I'd like to try doing it again."

"Well, we know that some parts of the industry are heading in that direction, but I don't see us necessarily going that way here."

"That's good to hear and I hope we don't, or at least not all the way across the board. But we see it happening all around. Some of the stations across town and in San Francisco are having reporters out shooting and cutting their own pieces and some of the photographers have been told to do the same or be cut loose. I like being ahead of the game. I'd like to be the one photographer the assignment desk can always depend on to be sent out, on my own, to pick up a story and write it, track it as a package and get it on the air all by myself."

Anzio mulled this over for a moment. I think I might have caught him a little off-guard with this idea. I'm sure that he also needed to see for himself that I could pull this off. And, frankly, after not having done it in twenty-five years, I needed to find that out as well.

Finally, he said, "Let's give it a try. Come up with a story and I'll make sure the assignment desk gives you time to go and shoot it and put it together. Then I'll take a look at it. If it's good enough, we'll put it on the news and go from there."

We shook hands on it and I headed out of his office with an entirely different feeling than I'd had fifteen minutes before when I went into his office. Now I was floating on air. The ball was entirely in my court to prove that I could do it.

The following week I pitched a story and was given the half-day needed to shoot it. It was a general news story, not specific to that day, so I wrote it and put it together over the rest of the week in between working on other assignments. I gave the story to Anzio and it ran on the news the next night without any alterations. After it aired Anzio came back into the E.N.G. editing area and gave me a high-five. It was the first package I'd worked on in my twenty years at KCRA where the reporter tag-out was, "I'm Mike Carroll, for KCRA-3 Reports." And I couldn't wait to do my next one.

Full Disclosure

I didn't grow up with printer's ink coursing through my veins. In high school I took a photography class and came away with one resolve: to earn my living with a camera.

I'm not an academic. I didn't go to college. I started in the mailroom. The route I took is not one I recommend. I'd probably be a lot farther in my career if I'd taken the traditional path and earned a degree. Everything I've learned about TV and journalism has been on-the-job.

Breaking Into TV News is an inside glimpse into TV news as I know it, based on nearly thirty years in the business. How I got my start and others got theirs, as well as how I shoot news and do my work as a reporter-photographer.

For the last two decades I've been at KCRA-TV in Sacramento, California. This book, however, is not about KCRA, its personnel, practices or policies. If you work for the competition and bought this book to pinpoint their weaknesses, I'm sorry to inform you that their only weakness is me. That said, if you want your money back you're going to have to list this book on eBay because you're not getting it from me.

Sometimes I wonder how I've managed to last this long. Most days I think to myself, "Well, they got their money's worth out of me today." Other days that same voice in my head mutters, "Who do you think you're fooling? Your days are numbered, amigo."

I attribute whatever success I've had to the same personality trait that got me through the door in the first place—attitude. I've found that simple things like maintaining a good attitude, smiling whenever possible, being agreeable with the people, ready to go when called and trying not to be difficult or demanding carry a lot of weight in the workplace.

Not to mention being able to shoot fast, edit faster and always make the deadline. If you're lucky enough to forge a pathway into this business, you'll find this out for yourself. And I sincerely hope you get the chance.

"The Business"

Working in TV news is commonly referred to as being "in the business."
News, as much as being a craft or profession, is a business. That's why it
pays. And it's a small group.

For almost thirty years I've watched journalism students pass through
newsroom doors on internships, spend a semester or two with us,
observing how real news is done, trying their hand at the job, maybe
putting together a demo reel to get a job after graduation. A few—a small
few—go on to careers in the business. A couple have even come back as
reporters and worked alongside me as colleagues.

Originally, this book was intended for students seeking real-world
insight into how to break into the business, and for people interested in
how the news works. Having the skills to be both a reporter and a
photographer is fast becoming a deal-breaking requirement for a reporter
position in entry-level stations and, increasingly, for many network news
reporter and producer positions. Even more importantly, I think it should
be read by the parents of those aspiring journalists so they can get an
unvarnished idea of just how demanding the business can be on their sons'
and daughters' lives.

For the vast majority of these students, their dreams of working in TV
never get any farther than their newsroom internship. After having spent
four or more years in college, taking every journalism class available—not
to mention having spent thousands of their dollars on tuitions, racking up
student loans—that's as close as most of them ever get.

Percentage-wise, the number of journalism interns who make it into this
business is below 10%, probably less than 5%. This gets down to individual
drive and initiative. TV stations don't set up booths on campuses recruiting
people to be on the news. You have to do all the work to get that first job,
and then the next one and the next. You have to get out there and work
every angle.

When you're finishing high school and looking at a college, ask how many graduates from that college actually went on to careers in journalism. And be sure to get the names of who they were so you can do follow-up e-mails to find out what they think of the education they got.

Because of programs like *60 Minutes, 20/20* and *Dateline,* many people think that everyone in TV news is an "Investigative Reporter." The truth is that most people working in TV news are just ordinary people covering regular stories in their communities.

Our work schedules, on the other hand, are not for the faint hearted. If having nights, weekends and national holidays off to hang out with family and friends is important for you, then news is not for you. While our jobs are also based on five-day work weeks, the days of the week and the shifts can be all over the place. News is a 365 days a year commitment. We work nights, early mornings, weekends and holidays—Thanksgiving, Christmas, New Year's, Easter, 4th of July, Labor Day—every day.

I was in the business for years before I had a Christmas off, and that was only because I'd slipped on some ice and injured my knee while covering a winter storm and the doctor ordered me off my feet for a week.

This extends to overtime. You could be wrapping up your shift when there's an earthquake, a tornado, plane crash, fire, shooting or police standoff that requires you to rush out and start broadcasting live. You could be on for two hours, ten hours or all night. It doesn't happen often, but it goes with the job. And pays the bills.

TV news departments post video stories to their websites along with text versions of the stories, just as newspapers are adding video stories to news copy on their websites. The divide between broadcasting and print is rapidly narrowing.

The public's attention spans are shorter. If a story isn't holding a viewer's interest, they hit the remote. Viewers in their thirties and younger are simultaneously surfing their iPhone's, iPad's or laptops. Many of today's youth are completely bypassing TV, getting *all* their information from their phones and the net.

Every news department across the country has scaled back—local and network television, newspapers, radio and Internet organizations. With more cable channels to compete with, the all-important advertising dollars are spread thin. News budgets have had to adjust, meaning consolidation— fewer people juggling more duties.

The only way to survive in broadcasting today is to make yourself invaluable. The bottom line in journalism is the written word. If you can write you are valued much higher on the newsroom ladder. Newsrooms across the country are consolidating and reporters are having to shoot their own stories. For photographers to survive, they must take up the pen and become reporters as well.

Many large market stations have taken a stand not to go the route of the one-person digital journalist, determined to maintain staffs—although, reduced in numbers—of reporter and photographer teams. Even so, nobody expects the status quo to remain forever. As senior reporters and photographers move on or retire, I find it difficult to believe that their positions won't gradually be replaced or augmented by multi-media journalists. It only makes financial sense. Stations can still have their star reporters, but can maintain bureaus and cover general assignment news and other beats with single-person digital journalists.

Change is inevitable and broadcasting is constantly shape-shifting with each new technological advance—from AM to FM radio, to TV, black & white to color, 16mm film to ¾" U-Matic video tape to Sony Betacam, and now to digitally-recorded High Definition. Recently I shot half of a story with an Android smart phone using the camcorder app.

One thing we can be certain of is that over the next couple of years TV news *will* be done differently. It's imperative to be able to adapt and change with it or start looking for another career. TV is a steamroller—you learn how to drive the machine or get run over by it.

The MMJ (Multi-Media Journalist), MMP (Multi-Media Producer), VJ (Video Journalist), DJ (Digital Journalist), Reporter-Photographer, whatever the job title, it is a position that has rapidly evolved. It is now a firm part of the broadcast journalism landscape and is only going to become more and more prevalent.

How I Got My Job

EVERYBODY IN TV HAS WAR STORIES about starting out at tiny, nothing stations in nowhere blips on the map.

When I started writing this section I thought it would just be a simple thumbnail overview of what it took for me to get into the business. However, once I got started, waves of memories and emotions came flooding back—all the hope, the optimism, the frustration, disappointment and struggle—and how victory was literally snatched from the jaws of defeat. Since so much of this book

I've always loved cameras. This 16mm Bolex was a joy to use, but expensive. I needed a job where I could use great cameras—and get paid.

is about the process of how to get a job and how to do the job, I thought it might be worthwhile to detail my personal experience in order to provide a small window into what it can be like to get your foot into such a competitive field.

As far as my story goes, while it worked for me, I don't recommend anybody try what I did. It was a last resort. Ironically, after getting in, I would be one of the first photographers at that station to begin winning awards for TV news photography.

If I was starting out today I'd purchase a DSLR camera, create a demo reel, post it to Youtube and Vimeo, and start freelancing my way in. Of course, a college degree wouldn't hurt, but even that has no guarantees.

To someone who's trying to get their first foot in the door the big question is, "How did you get your first job?"

Everybody's answer is different. What's mine?

"I lied my way in."

The Long Way 'Round

I grew up in St. Louis, Missouri, at that time a twelfth-size market. Cities and regions across the country are broken up into "media markets," based on the coverage area of radio and TV transmission towers. The larger the coverage area and the greater the population, the bigger the market size. And St. Louis was big.

Right out of high school I got a job in a camera store and bought a Nikon with dreams of being a photojournalist. I was also interested in film making. This was the time of Watergate and *60 Minutes* was one of the most-watched shows on television. Colleges were deluged with students majoring to be journalists and photojournalists. I've always had the belief that you learn-by-doing. I wanted to be working in news by the time they were graduating and starting to send out resumes.

Around this time I read a newspaper article about local TV news cameramen, which told how most had started out working in the mailroom for a year or two before moving up to the news department for another year or two and apprenticing as cameramen, eventually shooting news full-time.

I started making the rounds of the local TV stations, filling out employment applications. Getting no calls back, the following week I went back and filled the applications out again. A few days later, I did it again. Before long the receptionists had clipboards with applications ready when I came through the door. Eventually one of the receptionists got me an interview. A week later I was working in the mailroom.

I could hardly believe that I was working in the TV station that I grew up watching. The mailroom gave me a firsthand opportunity to see how every department worked, who everybody was and what they did. One time one of the news producers said to me, "You're always smiling. All day long you're always smiling. It's good to see someone who likes to be here."

One of the cameramen I got to know was Mike Dieffenbach, who would prove to have a major influence on my life. I was home watching the station's news one evening when a story came on and it was Mike's voice reporting the story. It was about Hannibal, Missouri, the small town north of St. Louis along the

Mike Dieffenbach framing up a 16mm CP-16 news camera in St. Louis in the 1980s.

Mississippi River where Samuel Clemens (a.k.a. Mark Twain) had grown up. Mike had pitched the story on a day when there was not much news to cover, so they cut him loose to go and do the story himself. For the managers it was nothing more than a way to keep him busy. For Mike it was an opportunity to exercise the storyteller in him. For me it was a revelation.

I told Mike how I was amazed that he'd done it all himself, then he told me that he'd majored in English at Princeton and made a documentary film as his thesis project. After graduation he used his film as a demo reel to get a job at a TV station in Colorado as a photographer-reporter. I'd never imagined that anyone could do both jobs of shooting and reporting at the same time, but it made perfect sense. TV news is about telling a story with pictures, so the best person to tell that story should be the one who's taking those pictures.

Up to this time TV news was still being shot on 16mm film. During my second year in the mailroom, videotape and portable recording decks were introduced and E.N.G. (Electronic News Gathering) hit with Richter scale impact. Overnight, film cameramen across the country were out the door and engineers with no photography background were sent out to shoot news. Suddenly having degrees in electronics and electrical engineering became a priority. The shooters at my station had foresight and their union had made a crossover arrangement. They were lucky and among the few who kept their jobs.

My world was turned upside down. I was at a complete loss about what to do. By this point, I knew I was never going to be a news shooter at that station. I was married and not getting any younger. I tried looking for jobs outside of TV but nothing else interested me. In time, I moved up into the Programming Department, spending my days in a light-proof closet, editing commercial breaks into movies. But this wasn't why I wanted to work in TV. The rules of the game had changed. I was going to have to change my game.

One day, my friend Mike Dieffenbach gave me some advice, "Look, trying to break into shooting news in this size market isn't going to happen any more. Why don't you do what I did—get a job in a smaller market, get your experience and then you can go wherever you want."

A producer friend helped me put together a media-oriented resume—two pages filled with smoke and mirrors—and a cover letter stressing my work experience in a TV station and eagerness to apply myself. I ran off fifty copies on the mailroom copy machine and started calling stations, moving out in every direction from St. Louis. Surprisingly, all the news directors or chief photographers took my calls. They were also unanimous in saying that I needed more experience. Interestingly, though, no one said anything about my lack of college education.

One evening I got home and my (then) wife said, "You've got a letter stamped return-to-sender addressed to some TV station in Cape Girardeau."

I'd been working from some old listings of TV stations and this one had apparently folded.

"What are you writing to them about?"

"Well, I . . . sent them a resume."

"For what? Are you looking for a job in Cape Girardeau? What for? To do what?"

"In the newsroom as a TV news cameraman."

This was the first she'd heard about any of this. I then came clean and told her what I'd been up to. She took this in slowly, finally asking, "So . . . . how many of these have you sent out?"

"Fifty."

"*Fifty!* You've sent out *fifty* resumes? Where?"

"Everywhere."

One day I was lamenting my lack of progress to Mike Dieffenbach when he said, "You know, when I was in Colorado I worked with a guy who got a job with even less experience than you."

"Really? How'd he do it?"

"He just put a couple of other people's stories together and put his name on it. Why don't you just grab a couple of my stories?"

That weekend I went into the newsroom early on a Saturday morning, when there was just a lone producer manning the police scanners. I went through the archives, armed with a list of some of Mike's more average stories that he thought I was capable of shooting, and dubbed them onto a tape. All I needed next was a station to mail "my resume tape" to.

I'd been working the phone for months, calling every station within 300 miles of St. Louis and had pushed out to the 400 mile mark when I dialed the listing for KWCH-TV in Hutchinson, Kansas. It turned out that the main offices had long since relocated to nearby Wichita and the Hutchinson offices were now being used as a satellite bureau, but I found myself talking to the Hutchinson anchor and reporter and right from the start I could feel this call was going to be different.

"Wow, this is a good time to call," she told me. "We've been the rock-bottom number-three station here for a long time, but we were just bought by some Kansas investors who want to turn the place around. They're pumping money into the place and hiring people. The reporters have always had to shoot their own stuff here, but now they're actually hiring photographers. Let me give you the number of our news director, Steve Ramsey, and tell him that I told you to call."

I paused just long enough to get my breath, then dialed the number she gave me.

"This is Steve Ramsey," came the authoritative voice at the other end of the line. He then jumped into telling me the same story about the changes taking place at KWCH and their determination to reinvent the station into a strong, competitive news organization. He said he'd just filled a number of photographer positions, but had one left. "I've got a couple people I'm looking at, but send me your tape and I'll look at it."

I later found out that Steve Ramsey had worked at KWCH-TV as a photographer-reporter in his early twenties before going on to KFOR-TV in Oklahoma City, a station that was awarded N.P.P.A. (National Press Photographers Association) TV News Photography Station of the Year during the time he was there. He'd also worked alongside Darrel Barton, a man who had twice been named the N.P.P.A. TV News Photographer of the Year and would later become one of the creative forces behind CBS' *48 Hours*, along with Dan Rather. Steve was the embodiment of news—a no-nonsense guy who could do anything. Yet, his greatest talent was in being able to work with people and motivate them to be better than they thought they could be.

I finished the call in a near state of euphoria. I'd made two calls in a matter of minutes and both had been positive and encouraging. I knew I shouldn't get my hopes up, but it was too late. This sounded like the perfect place—a station that was hungry to prove itself, just like me.

I wrote "Mike Carroll" across "my" tape in big, bold Magic Marker, and sent it off. That night I excitedly told my wife.

"Where is it?"

"In Kansas."

"Where in Kansas?"

"I don't know."

A Month of Agony

A week passed and I was on pins and needles the whole time. Not having heard anything, I called Steve Ramsey back under the guise of making sure he'd received "my" tape.

"It was okay. Nothing great."

Then he paused a moment before continuing, "I have to be honest with you, Mike, I offered the position to a photographer up in Nebraska last night and he accepted. He's been working up there for a couple years and he has a lot more experience than you. I'm sorry, I know that's not what you wanted to hear. I know what it's like to be disappointed."

"No, no, I understand. You need to get the best people you can find."

"Would you like me to send your tape back to you?"

"No," I said determinedly. "I like what I've heard about what you're doing at your station and if you have anything else open up I'd appreciate it if you'd keep me in mind."

"Well, Mike, I like your attitude. I'll do that."

It was nothing that I hadn't expected. But on the positive side, a news director had finally considered me and taken me seriously. I learned that I had to sell myself in order to make up for my lack of experience.

The following week I was working in the film department when the phone rang.

"Mike Carroll, this is Steve Ramsey in Wichita."

"Mr. Ramsey," I said, never expecting to hear his voice again. "How are you?"

"I'm fine. Look, Mike, the reason I'm calling is I've got another job opening. Well, actually it's the same job opening. The guy in Nebraska changed his mind and didn't take the job after all, so the job's open again. I have to be honest, I have a couple of candidates that I'm looking at who have more experience than you, but I like your attitude and wanted to know if you're still interested?"

"Yes—yes, sir, absolutely."

"All right, I'm glad to hear it. Like I said, I'm talking to a few other people but I'll get back to you in a week or two."

"All right, thank you, Mr. Ramsey. Thank you."

For the first time a news director had called *me*—and it was my attitude and not my experience that had impressed him. More than ever I wanted to work for this man.

Another long week of waiting. My wife and I didn't dare whisper a word about this to anyone—not family, friends, anyone—not wanting to set ourselves up for disappointment. Yet, in spite of the odds against me, seeds of hope were starting to take hold.

I got on the phone again. Once again, Ramsey had offered the job to another photographer who was working at a station in Iowa. And once again, the photographer hadn't immediately accepted and was thinking about it. Ramsey told me to call him back in a couple days.

"Mike, how're you holding up?"

"I'm hanging in there."

"Good, glad to hear it. Well, the guy in Iowa passed, but I offered it to another guy last night up in Des Moines. He said he had to talk it over with his wife. If he doesn't take it, are you still interested?"

"Yes, sir. Yes, I am. I really like the time you've taken to talk to me and appreciate you considering me. I know I don't have the experience you're looking for, but I really want to work there for you."

"Well, Mike, I like your attitude. This is what I'm going to do, I'm going to have my chief photographer call you at home tonight and have the two of you talk. How does that sound?"

Now I was really on edge. It had been one thing talking with news directors, but talking to the chief news photographer—he'd see through me like glass.

That evening I was in the kitchen of our little apartment when the phone rang and it was KWCH chief photographer Jim Anderson. He'd looked over "my" tape and talked to me in detail about each story and how they did things differently there—no panning, no zooming, greater emphasis on the use of natural sound to tell the story, and that while he hated tripods he also hated shaky shots. Frankly, I didn't understand most of what he was saying.

Finally, he talked about my resume and that I hadn't gone to college.

"No, I started working right out of high school. Things were kind of tight around home and, to be honest, if I hadn't I don't think my parents would still be in their house."

"Well, that sounds like it was the right thing to do then, doesn't it? I didn't go to college either. I went into the Army for six years, then the Air Force for another six, where I learned communications and video. So that won't be a problem around here."

That was a response that I never expected to hear.

"Now I know you don't have that much experience. If we take you on I want you to ride around with me for a couple days and observe what I do. You sound like a nice young man and if Steve Ramsey decides to go with you, then I think you'll do just fine." He

KWCH chief photographer Jim Anderson on The Great Wall of China while on a special assignment covering the Kansas governor's visit in 1984.

said that with a tone of confidence that gave me confidence as well. For the first time, I allowed myself to think, "This might actually happen."

The following Tuesday, I returned to the film department after lunch to find a message to call Steve Ramsey. I took a phone into my editing booth and closed the door so no one could hear.

"Mike, thanks for calling me back. I just wanted you to know that I talked to Jim Anderson and he said you two had had a good talk. We both wish you had more experience, but Jim feels that if we do decide to go with you he can make a pretty good shooter out of you."

"Thank you, that's what I want, too."

"I know you do. Look, I still haven't gotten a definite decision from that guy up in Des Moines, but I need to get this position filled. Call me tomorrow morning at 10:30 and I'll have a decision for you one way or the other."

I was right on the edge of it actually happening, yet it could also mean the door being closed in my face for good. It was a miserable night. I couldn't eat and there wasn't an ounce of conversation in me. I was just passing time until the next morning.

The station had a long list of pickups and deliveries to what seemed like every ad agency and TV station in town. But before I could get to their business I needed to take care of mine and swung by the apartment a couple of blocks away. My wife was reorganizing the kitchen pantry while I nervously sat down at the kitchen table. "Time to get this over with." With trembling fingers, I picked up the phone and dialed long distance to Wichita for the last time.

"Hello. Newsroom."

"Steve Ramsey, please."

"Steve's in a meeting right now. You want me to have him call you back?"

"Uh, sure. Just tell him Mike Carroll called and I'll call him back later."

"Oh, he said you'd be calling. Hold on."

Then I was put on hold. I sat there knowing full well what he was going to tell me and wondering why I'd ever put myself through this. Then there was a click on the other end of the phone and the full-bodied voice of Steve Ramsey boomed over the line.

"Mike Carroll, how the hell are you? I talked to the guy in Des Moines last night and the son-of-a-bitch's wife won't move. So what the hell—come on out to Wichita. You got the job!"

My stomach about fell out of me. "What? Thank you. Thank you, Mr. Ramsey."

"All right. I'm sorry, I've got to finish up this goddamn meeting. Give me your number there and I promise I'll call you back in fifteen minutes."

As I gave him the number my wife was looking at me from across the kitchen, her mouth gaping open. "You got the job?"

"I got it. Start packing." I never felt more shocked in my life.

It was almost impossible to believe. I'd gotten the job that I wanted at the station where I wanted to work. It had nothing to do with experience, just sheer determination and keeping a positive attitude throughout.

When I got back to the station I quit my job, giving two days' notice. That Friday night when I got home from my last day of work my wife had the car packed. I just had to make one last long distance call to Kansas. The Wichita station had a trade-out arrangement with one of the downtown hotels where new employees could stay free for a few days during their transition. A clerk at the front desk answered.

"Hello, I'm driving to your hotel from St. Louis."

"Yes, sir. How can I help you?"

"How do I get there?"

A few years later I got to know Rich Carlson, the chief photographer at KRON-TV in San Francisco, who had been runner-up to being the 1986 N.P.P.A. TV News Photographer of the Year. While all the other N.P.P.A. photographers were shooting everything on tripods and using static shots, Rich was shooting hand held, zooming and moving around. He had a totally original eye that I could only quantify as being "California cool." But then Rich was a surfer, so it was only fitting.

He would send me his tapes to study and I would send him my work to be critiqued. A terrific guy who was always bubbling with enthusiasm and positive vibes. From the first moment I met him I wanted to be like him.

He'd started out as an editor at KRON, but he longed to get out on the street and shoot. His dilemma, just like mine, was that San Francisco was a top-10 market, so there was no way he could break in there.

"So what did you do?" I asked.

"I was an editor so I just put a couple stories on a tape and put my name on it and mailed it out. Got a job shooting up in Oregon. I wasn't fooling anybody. They know when you're doing it. But it was a different time then and you had to do what you had to do. Besides, either you worked out or they'd cut you. I worked out."

As I was writing this chapter, I was curious to know where Steve Ramsey was. I couldn't imagine him not being involved in news somewhere. I Googled his name and was shocked to discover that he'd passed away in 2005 at the age of 52. It was unfathomable to me that this lion of a man who'd given me a chance and a career was no longer with us. Without him, I don't know where I'd be today.

Steve lived, ate, slept news. He'd done everything and knew how it all worked. Every now and then when a big story was breaking, he'd hand the newsroom over to his assistant news director, jump into his pick-up and drive out to the scene. Sometimes he'd even ask to borrow your news camera and shoot some of the story. He was a leader who led by example. As long as you were always trying your best, he was always willing to help you.

It's a sadder business without him in it. He was the best boss I've ever had and the best news director I've ever known.

INTERNSHIPS

KCRA Spring 2012 interns—Ashley Gordon, San Joaquin Delta College, Stockton (left), Britney Sweis, American River College, Sacramento (center), and Amanda Clark, California State University, Sacramento (right).

KCRA reporter intern Mark Lewis, American River College, Sacramento.

EVERY SEMESTER JOURNALISM STUDENTS from community colleges and universities pour into TV newsrooms across the country as interns with aspirations of being reporters, anchors and producers. A relative few interns give thought to being photographers and, from my experience, the reporter interns who are aware that they're going to have to be reporter-photographers on their first jobs never ask technical questions regarding cameras and how to recording audio.

Internships grant you access to a newsroom for a semester and you can usually apply for a second semester to get a more advanced experience. However, unless you've been able to build friendships with people within the newsroom, once the second semester is over and the access expires, those doors could be closed to you forever.

Before registering at a community college or university make sure they offer an internship program with one of the local news organizations. If they don't, contact the local stations and ask if they offer independent internships and how to apply.

Most stations have an interview process when considering students for internships. Treat this the same as a job interview—come prepared and be professionally dressed. First impressions make a difference. It's also not a bad idea to have a resume and samples of your work.

All newsrooms are different. Some regard interns as nuisances. Others treat them as free labor, putting them to work answering phones. A few stations have structured programs designed to give the students the best learning opportunities possible, but these are not the norm.

The college internship is generally the *only* opportunity toward finding a career in journalism. Whether the goal is to work in radio, TV, newspapers, Internet, etc.—an internship is the *one* chance to get real news experience to put on a resume to break into the business.

Entry-level TV stations work on extremely limited budgets. By necessity they have to do much more with less. Job applicants must be versatile and be able to be their own reporter, producer, writer, photographer and editor—not to mention sending in web stories, iPhone photos and tweets throughout the day. Accept this or change your major and get into something else.

Act Like A Professional

The people in the newsroom are not your friends, they are professionals working for a living. Conduct yourself as an adult. At all times regard the internship as an audition for employment.

- Be nice. Smile. You don't have to bring people coffee or make cookies. (Although, if you make good cookies and bring a platter to the newsroom, you'll be noticed.)
- Listen. Pay attention. Don't chatter idly. Choose your words carefully and keep answers brief. You're not there to participate in conversations. You're there to observe and learn.
- Carry a notepad and take notes.
- Say "Yes" and "Yes, sir." "No, ma'am." "Please." "Thank you." Not "Yeah."
- Speak clearly. Don't mumble. Enunciate your syllables.
- Remove the word "like" from your speech. Avoid trendy slang.
- Dress professionally. Prepare for the job you want to have. Wear a suit or something nice, casual.
- Do yourself a favor and go to a Brooks Brothers or Ann Taylor Outlet Store and let a clothing advisor choose professional clothes for you.
- Don't wear trendy clothes or flashy shoes that you'd go clubbing in. You could be out in the rain, snow, a muddy field or the city dump. Keep a bag in your car packed with something suitable for any situation.
- Speak in an adult voice. Newscasters do not have high-pitched, squeaky voices. Use a deeper tone of voice. (If you don't have one, start working on one now.)

Read and Be Informed

Be up-to-date on current events. Don't just watch the news—read newspapers. Most reporters, producers, writers and assignment editors make a point to scan the local papers for story ideas before coming in to work. You need to adopt the same frame of mind.

One of the first things I do every morning is check out the *Los Angeles Times* (latimes.com) and the *New York Times* (nytimes.com), which I also check throughout the day on my smart phone. For an alternate perspective of world and U.S. news I visit the U.K. paper *The Guardian* (guardian.co.uk).

Being well-informed in local and national events will make an impression.

Follow The Pros—Try It Yourself

Get copies of scripts. Learn the formatting of a TV news story. It's shorter than you'd expect.

Go out with the crews. When the reporter shoots a stand-up, ask if you can shoot one as well. Time permitting, the reporter and photographer, or reporter-photographer, will usually be generous and will offer helpful criticism and inside tricks of the trade.

Watch how the reporter logs the footage and writes the script. Once the reporter finishes writing, ask if you can have a copy of the script.

Ask to go with the reporter into the audio booth and see how an audio track is recorded. Everyone thinks that cutting a track is simply reading into the mic. Nothing could be farther from the truth. When someone cuts a track they have to be stronger, louder and bolder than they are in regular conversation. It's more like doing a dramatic reading. The reporter has to punch up selected words to emphasize points of the story to the viewers at home.

KCRA intern Naomi Lee learns how to use Avid to edit her resume reel. Naomi is one of the smart people who turned her internship into a part-time job to get her foot in the door. She continued working on her reel, making contacts, and during the writing of this book, went on to become a full-time producer at KSBW in Salinas, California.

Ask to sit in with the photographer or editor (some stations only have editors for cutting stories). Watch how the footage is edited into a story. Most students think TV news is all about reporting, but their first job will invariably require them to edit their stories as well.

After the package is completed, ask to copy the footage onto your own hard drive so that you can write, track and edit your own version of the story for your audition reel.

- Log the interviews, write your own script and track it. Don't just grab the reporter's finished script and track their words.
- Learn how to edit and cut your stories yourself.
- Show it to the reporter and get their feedback.
- The first sign of being a professional is to be able to accept criticism.

- Get feedback on your editing. You'll probably get suggestions about using different shots from the ones you've selected to make your story more effective.
- Write and edit a number of stories to create a demo reel.
- Post your work on your website.
- Don't be passive. Show initiative, without being aggressive.
- Use the time preciously. It's over before you know it.
- Don't let yourself get stuck in the newsroom. Get out into the field—that's where news happens.

KCRA intern Nha Nguyen learning how to shoot her own stand-up as a one-person journalist. From her internship, Nha has gone on to reporting at KEZI-TV in Eugene, Oregon.

The feedback that I remember is about the superficial stuff—about the hair and the clothes and the make-up, which I found very important. I remember doing an anchor demo and a female anchor saying, "I wouldn't wear lip gloss because it's distracting. And I'd wear something that has a collar," because I was wearing a dress that didn't have a collar. And she was right—the next time I did a demo, it looked much better. It's important to wear clothes that are timeless and professional.

    Lilian Kim, KGO-TV, San Francisco

I find that most interns think a stand-up is improvised and it's easy and they don't go to the effort to write it out ahead of time.

    They have a very tough time. I have to tell them what to do. It's very rare to find one who's driven enough. A lot of them don't make the most of their time. They just sit around and wait for things to happen. They're not aggressive. And those are the people that make me think, "They're going to drop out and pursue something else," because they don't have the personality for it.

    Anonymous Quote

KCRA intern Nha Nguyen shoots a stand-up for incoming-intern Alexandria Backus, CSU Stanislaus, Turlock

Get A Camera On Your Shoulder

Reporter interns have to accept that their first job, or couple of jobs, are going to be as MMJ, requiring them to be their own photographer as well. However, while they will spend time with reporters to develop their writing skills and in the editing room learning how to cut stories, they almost never will put a camera on their shoulder and do any shooting.

Recently I had this conversation with an intern: "So how's your reel coming?"

KCRA intern Rachel Behrmann gets comfortable with the 25 pound Sony XDCAM news camera.

"My reel's finished and I did all the writing and I edited all the stories myself."

"Great. Did you shoot any of them yourself?"

"No. But I know how to shoot."

Many interns, who haven't done any shooting, have confidently said these exact words: "Oh, I know how to shoot." This is pretty amazing to me because I've been shooting for thirty years and I'm still learning how to use a camera.

Understanding the distinction between a long shot, a medium shot and a close-up *does not* mean that you're going to know how to shoot those shots or be able to understand how to frame them up properly in the viewfinder when it's happening live in front of you.

Shooting is about **attention to detail**. Having a close-up on one object, yet making sure that there aren't two or three other objects in the shot as well that will make the picture confusing. Or grabbing an establishing shot of a building with someone walking by in front, and it isn't until you get back to the station and you're editing it that you realize that the person is picking their nose or subtly giving you the finger.

If you can get a news director to look at your reel, expect to be asked, "How much of this did you shoot yourself?" If your answer is, "None of it," then expect to be asked, "Why not?"

Shooting a story on independent filmmakers with my own Panasonic DVX 100A.

The MMJ Shooting Challenge

Get out of the newsroom and into the field with an MMJ or reporter and photographer crew every chance you get. After you've been out a few times, start taking a camcorder or DSLR camera that records HD video along with you and shoot your own B-roll, and a few quick interviews if you can.

Most interns have the idea that they have to shoot a regular news camera for their reel in order to be taken seriously. Nothing could be farther from the truth. In the rapidly changing landscape of TV news where stations will be using $50,000 Sony HD XDCAMs right alongside $3,000 Sony HD camcorders and even footage shot with an Apple iPhone—all in the same story—there is no longer a defining standard as to what a news camera is. As of this writing I am shooting with a Sony XDCAM, but I have also shot stories with Sony, Panasonic and JVC camcorders, as well as with my own personal Canon 7D, and even an Android smartphone—and *all* of them have been broadcast on the news.

So grab a news camera if one is available to you, and if not then bring one of your own and take advantage of the opportunity to shoot side by side with a professional. Then later have your footage critiqued shot-by-shot by the MMJ or photographer. You'll be surprised at what they see that you never picked up on.

Strive to have at least one story on your resume reel be one that you have entirely reported, shot and edited yourself and make note of this on your website. Believe me, news directors will take notice of this and it will make you stand out from the pack.

Do An Internship Early—Make Sure This Is For You

Many journalism majors put off doing their internships until the final semester, or even after graduation, using the reasoning, "Because I wanted to be as prepared as I could so that I could take full advantage of the experience."

Frankly, I think that's a big mistake. Too often these eager-to-be-anchors have built up fantasy images of what television is and how news works. They've put all their focus on academics and are not prepared for the real world of running from one story to another, constant web-update deadlines, and what it takes to simply get stories on the air. I've seen more than a few go back to the registration office to sign up for Masters Degrees in Business or Marketing or anything except news.

Nurturing News Directors

News directors are always looking for talent. If they recognize an eager, hard-working intern as having potential they may even help them get that first job. It's a small world and news directors know each other. News directors in larger markets have been known to call news directors at entry-level stations to recommend a student worth looking at, then follow that young person's progress so see if their initial hunch was right. That former student's second or third job could wind up bringing them full circle right back to that first newsroom where their internship was.

I've worked with several reporters who started out as interns coming out on stories with me (and who I probably should have been nicer to) who went on to get jobs in tiny, unheard-of markets for a year or two, only to come marching right back to my station as full-fledged reporters, working alongside me as colleagues. Perhaps they missed the abuse I gave them.

Turn An Internship Into A Job

Internships can also be an entryway into your first news job. Making a good impression, showing ability and competence, students frequently segue directly from their internship into entry-level positions as writers, video editors and working on the assignment desk in the very newsroom where they were interning. These jobs generally

Former student, then intern, and now KCRA photographer Steve Gonzales.

require working nights, early mornings and weekends, but they get your foot in the door and draw a paycheck.

An overnight or weekend position as a writer can lead to producing and on into management. I know of one intern who followed this career path and in a few short years was offered a position as a news director.

Several years ago I spoke to a broadcast journalism class at Sacramento State University. Afterward, Steve Gonzales, one of the students, told me how much he wanted to do the kind of work that I do for a living. A few months later he was in the E.N.G. Department on an internship, which led to a job as an overnight editor. With his foot in the door, he started borrowing gear and shooting news stories on his own to get experience and show that he was capable of doing more. He displayed eagerness and initiative. Steve has how been a fellow news cameraman at KCRA for years, and he continues to show that he can do more, occasionally filling in as a reporter-photographer.

Making Your Own Road

At this point you might be asking: "Hey, Mike, you didn't go to college but you got a job in TV. If you can do it, why can't I?" And I would respond: "Maybe you can." It would take a lot of determination and guts and you have to be willing to move anywhere. But you might make it. Going the traditional college route is no guarantee of a job in news, but it can greatly speed up the process.

There are plenty of other avenues into the business. The U.S. military offers outstanding journalism training. Many veterans go directly from the service into good-paying civilian sector journalism jobs.

If I was starting out today I'd either go the military route or sign up for classes at a community college as a means to getting an internship. Once I was interning in a news department, I'd work at building relationships and putting together a tape that I'd post to Youtube and Vimeo. I'd start working the internet to find a job anywhere in the country that would take me. You can always go back and finish school later. I know many people who started working in newsrooms while still in college and had full-time jobs long before they graduated. I also know people who, once they'd worked their way into newsroom careers, left school behind.

Other people who are savvy with the Internet are forging their own routes completely independently as freelancers. For a few thousand dollars they'll buy a camera, microphones, laptop and editing software to create videos, post them to Youtube and Vimeo and to their own websites. They can reach out to news organizations without ever setting foot inside a newsroom. It then gets down to applying their skills, both professional and at building relationships, to be able to work their way into a regular job at a TV station.

It would not be the most direct route, but I definitely see this as a pathway that many of the next digital journalists will take. Also, as college tuitions continue to escalate, these alternate avenues could become increasingly appealing to some aspiring journalists. The traditional route of the college internships is still the most common and reliable roadmap into the business. But that does not have to be the only road. For others, the road less taken may be a little longer and a bit harder, but it could be the right road for them.

The Resume Website

The Internet has changed everything in our lives and news is in the forefront of this. News directors are no longer interested in audition reels on DVDs or paper resumes that clutter up a work space. In fact, if you're still using the regular mail to get into TV news, that could work against you. News directors could get the impression that you're not up to speed with technology—and TV news has always been about technology.

If you contact a news director by phone or by e-mail, they don't want to wait a few days for your reel to arrive in the mail—they want to see it while they're on the phone with you or by clicking a link to an e-mail that will take them immediately to your website to see what you've got to offer—*now*.

The Resume Reel

If you're going to be a reporter or a photographer in TV news—and in the case of this book you're going to be both—you have to have a "Resume Reel," often still referred to as a "Resume Tape," even though videotape itself hasn't been manufactured for years.

A reel runs from six to eight minutes and should begin with a series of stand-ups, typically shot when an intern is out shadowing an MMJ or a reporter+photographer crew. After the reporter has shot a stand-up or done a live shot, they will frequently pass the microphone to the intern so they can try their hand at it.

If you haven't gone the intern route, or you think you can improve on the stand-ups you already have, there's nothing to prevent you from shooting new ones with your own camcorder or DSLR. Just make sure to use a good mic so the sound is clean.

This should be followed by three scripted, tracked and edited packages. Most people put   these together during their internships, using footage shot by a photographer or the reporter-photographer. This is invaluable experience because you can get feedback on your writing, editing and shooting from professionals who do it for a living. The more determined interns will strive to have a completed reel by the end of their second internship.

What News Directors Look For

The purpose of a reel is to show a news
director who you are and what you can
do. A news director is only going to look
at your reel for the first 20 seconds to a
minute. If he or she doesn't see anything
that grabs them in that time then it's on
to the next one—and there are always
plenty of next ones.

If a news director likes what they see
they'll keep watching to see how well
you can tell a story. If you make it
through the first round, it's usually the
second round where you're eliminated—
in the writing and the story telling.
Being able to draw an audience in with
words and present facts in a dramatic
and compelling way—being a *writer*—is
one of the rarest talents in the business.

If you make it through this second
round, that's when a news director looks
at the resume, which has either been e-
mailed or is posted on your website. The
resume essentially has only one real
value—it lists a phone number and e-
mail contact information. Nothing else
on the page matters—whether you have
a PhD from Harvard or you've never
finished community college. All that
matters is whether you've got the goods.

Frames from the stand-up montage of
KCRA intern Nha Nguyen's resume reel,
which got her a job as a reporter at KEZI-TV
in Eugene, Oregon.

I purchased my name as a domain name, ashleighwalters.com, because I knew a website would be a necessity for the future.

I visited reporter Wayne Freedman in San Francisco while I was on vacation there and Wayne introduced me to Kevin Keeshan, the news director at KGO. I brought a tape and he watched it and said, "I think this is great. I want to tell some people about you. Where's your website?" And I said, "Well, the domain name has been purchased but it just hasn't been launched yet." So the moment I got home the website had to go live—and I made it happen.

You have to have it ready when people ask for it. You can't say, "Oh yeah. Give me two months and I'll get my friends to work on that for me." You have to be able to build it yourself and get it done and update it. If a news director says, "I need to see more of your ability to enterprise a story," you have to be able to provide it—and provide it quickly.

I think that we are seeing the last gasping breaths of the DVD resume. The job that I have now at WPTV in West Palm Beach, Florida, was by word of mouth and people recommending me. I didn't send any resume tapes to anybody. But, through the website, people pass your name around and say, "Oh, have you seen this person?" Or, "We have this opening, do you know of anybody?" And they'll say, "Oh, I know Ashleigh Walters. Here's her website." The link is forwarded on and people can instantly see you. People can Google my name to find it. It just eliminates so much of the delay.

News directors have a busy schedule. If they have five minutes to look at you, don't waste their time. Connect them to your videos with the simple click of a button. The same sense of urgency that we put into delivering news to our viewers should also apply to maintaining our websites."

ASHLEIGH WALTERS, WPTV-TV, West Palm Beach, Florida

Start A Website—Market Yourself

Everyone should register their name as a .com and own it as a registered domain name. Whether you want to be in news or sell real estate or collect model trains, you should own your name as a web domain. I tried to register my name but it was already taken, so I registered mikecarrollfilms.com. The Internet is where everything is going—business, entertainment, education, information, social networking, etc. It's important to be a part of it and embrace it.

Register your website in your name so that it's easy to find. If your name is "Jane Smith" then register your domain name as "janesmith.com." If that's taken, then register a simple variation that's relevant to your career ambitions, such as "janesmithnews.com," "janesmithtvnews.com," or "janesmithreporter.com." (I'd hold off on "janesmithnetworkanchor.com" for now.) Don't try to be clever by calling it "thisisjanesmithswebsite.com" because no one will be able to find it.

If you haven't registered your name yet, put this book down, go to your computer and buy your domain name *now*.

Maintain Your Site Yourself

Many people start out with a simple web-building site that offers ready-made templates for their professional resume and bio, where they can attach (or "embed") Youtube clips of their work and so on.

This is fine for beginners, but keep in mind that there are hundreds of people who you will be competing with in the job market who also have beginner sites like this. You need to make your site stand out.

Some people who are afraid of the web or don't feel they're web-savvy enough hire a person to build and maintain a site for them. That's a big mistake. A website needs to be regularly updated and added to. Other people are not going to be as committed to your site and it will be costly to pay someone to update your site as often as you're going to need.

Also, news directors are impressed by people who understand the Internet and social media and have some working knowledge of how websites work. Every news organization on the planet has a website and journalists are expected to publish stories to webs and update them throughout the day. If you're already comfortable with working on the web—and perhaps even have ideas on how to improve a station's site—that could make the difference between a news director hiring you over another candidate.

Take The Time To Get Your Site Right

Building a website takes time. It's not rocket science but, like Rome, you can't build a decent one in a day.

I first entered the worldwide web (www.) with a .Mac site, which was as easy as a right click of the mouse here and there to create pages, text, and drag and drop photos. Another click and everything was instantly published for the world to see—or at least the handful of people who knew I existed. But this helped me to overcome my intimidation of web design.

A few years later, in preparation for the publication of my first book, I knew that I needed to have a more professional website. I studied the sites that I visit regularly and noticed that they were all designed using WordPress (wordpress.com and wordpress.org), an open-source platform for creating websites that allows individual customization of a site's look and layout with thousands of different free downloadable theme templates to choose from. There are plenty of how-to books available and step-by-step tutorials on Youtube to help build or modify almost any kind of WordPress site you'd want. The method is a bit more complicated than what I started out with, but it's given me the high-end look that I wanted.

To get the new WordPress version of my website close to the way I wanted it to look took almost three months with lots of trial and error involved—but that's all part of the creative process. As of this writing **mikecarrollfilms.com** has been online for over two years and I'm still tinkering with it. However, every time I tweak something the site gets better.

(Note: This is not an endorsement for WordPress, it's just what I know and use and works for me. You have to find what works best for you.)

Promote Yourself With A Blog

I encourage people to have a "blog-driven" website where the blog is the "home" page, and not a site where the first thing you see is a "welcome" page that reads, "Welcome to Jane Smith's website." This is formulaic and unimaginative.

The purpose of a website is to introduce yourself to potential employers.

You are the product so you need to sell people on *you*. Write a blog about your journey and have your most recent post be the first thing that greets people on your "home" page. If they like the first post, they'll continue to check out the older ones. With each new post you're giving potential employers a reason to keep coming back and monitoring your development.

Fill your blog with video stories you've done, photos of yourself as a working professional, and updates about new things you're learning. If you're still in school, blog about what things you're learning, post videos of your work and write about how you're improving. If you've graduated, post about any new projects you're working on, journalism conferences you're attending, volunteer organizations you're involved with. News directors are impressed by volunteer work because it shows involvement in your community.

A blog is like a diary that you're sharing with the public. It doesn't have to be long and involved, just a few paragraphs or so written in a casual, yet professional, conversational style. Always display a positive attitude, with a touch of humor. It's also not a bad idea to occasionally post something about your dog or cat or recent trip to show the human side of you.

I post all of my reporter-photographer stories to Youtube or Vimeo, embed them on my website and post them on Facebook to get the word out to as many people as possible. I also try to include a background blog on how the stories were done.

This also serves as a backup video library. When one of my hard drives crashed, I lost a lot of my library of stories. Fortunately, I was able to download much of my work back off of Youtube and Vimeo, although, in lower resolution.

Keep Your Site Upbeat & Positive

Do not use your blog as a platform to vent on a situation or express personal animosities. This extends to Facebook, Twitter, texting and whatever other social media that leaves a trail that could be used against you. This turns people off, could damage your career or get you fired. If you have nothing good to say, then don't post it on the Internet.

The Internship's Over—Keep Working At It

The internship's over. You're out of school. You have your website with your audition stories posted on it. You're working the phone, calling news directors, sending out thank you notes. In the meantime you're waiting tables, bagging groceries, working temp jobs—biding your time until you get your break into the business.

That's not enough. You need to keep working at it. News directors always want to know, "What have you done lately?"

When you're talking with a news director the question may come up, "So when did you put your reel together?"

"During my internship."

"So your reel is over a year old? What have you been doing in the meantime?"

"Well, I had to complete school and I've been looking for a job."

"So, this is the same reel you've had for a year now? Is there anything you've done recently?"

If more than a year has passed since a reel was completed news directors may feel that it's gotten stale, you're not keeping yourself current and you don't want it enough. They're looking for individuals with drive. Continuing to find new stories and posting them to the Internet shows a passion for the work, as well as the initiative to pick up a camera and do whole projects on your own.

Just because you're not in a TV station with access to professional gear is no excuse. You have to treat your reel as a living thing. It has to be updated and added to, which is another reason why having a website is so important—so that you can continue to do new stories to show your development and initiative. Invest in yourself and keep improving. Buy a DSLR camera or camcorder and easy-to-use editing software and continue to add new stories to your body of work, as well as tweak and improve the existing reel.

If you see a fire or an accident or tree branches snapping off in the wind, shoot some pictures or video with your iPhone, call the local TV stations and e-mail them in. And while you're shooting that newsworthy scene, turn the iPhone around on yourself and shoot a stand-up, send it in to the TV stations and add it to your reel. Keep developing your on-air presence.

If you need a subject for a story, small businesses and non-profits always need publicity. You can do an independent news story that you can post on your website and they can embed to their website and it's a win-win.

When you post new material to your website, send out e-mail updates to the news directors you've made contact with. News directors like people with perseverance, strong work ethics, and who don't throw in the towel.

Three personality traits that news directors respond to:
- Positive Attitude
- Self-Motivated
- Initiative

THE PROFESSIONALS

KCRA news director Anzio Williams (far right) oversees an afternoon producers meeting.

Everyone in TV news finds their own path into the business. To provide a wide array of experiences and perspectives, I spoke with a number of other people in the business—some of whom I've known and worked with and others who came recommended to me—to find out their stories. Most followed the traditional route of college and internships, then starting in small stations and working their way up. Some are still working in the field. Others have moved up into management. All started out as interns. Two are now in positions to give people a chance at being professionals.

Some of the books I've learned the most from contain collections of interviews with people about their lives, what they do and how they do it. I hope the next series of chapters will be as useful and inspirational for you.

ANZIO WILLIAMS: News Director, KCRA-TV, Sacramento, California

His interest in journalism is equaled only by his interest in helping students of journalism, frequently speaking to classes and staying in touch with talented students to help them pursue their dreams. I've seen him working with interns on their resume reels and getting on the phone to help them find their first jobs. Not to mention letting a cameraman with a few decades of experience cross over and report his own packages.

Anzio used his own college internship to work himself into a job on the newsroom assignment desk, and from there into producing, and rapidly up the ladder to news director. Less than a year into being the news director at WDSU-TV in New Orleans, he saw his newsroom and entire TV station overtaken by the waters of Hurricane Katrina. But he still found a way to get the news out. Television news is a passion for him, as is a willingness to help other young people with hopes and ambitions, just as he once had, to get their foot into the working world of broadcasting.

What got you interested in news?

We only had one television in the household and my grandmother was a big news watcher, so I watched the news with her. I remember being on the floor, doing my homework, and watching Walter Cronkite.

Then in my third grade class a producer and an anchor visited and I just continued paying attention to it, saying, "I like this news thing."

As a high school football player, the father of one of my teammates was a TV reporter and every time I'd see him I'd think, "That's a TV reporter," and I'd ask him a lot of questions.

We had a pretty good football team so the sports guys and camera guys would always come out, and I was just always fascinated with what they were doing, what they were shooting, and what would actually make it on TV. And I would say that I'm still just as fascinated about what we do now as I was even then.

I got a chance to visit a television station when I was in high school, the ABC-affiliate in Durham, North Carolina, and I was in love—I was in *love* with it.

When I was in college, in the middle of my freshman year I got a job in the circulation department of the *Greensboro News & Record* newspaper. I would sneak up to the sports department on Friday nights because I liked the action of watching them covering Friday night football. Then I'd go in on Saturdays during football season when they were out covering sports because I wanted to be around newsgathering. I figured out pretty quickly that I didn't want to go the newspaper route. My adrenalin was still pumping and going, but it wasn't like it was when I was in a television station.

I did an internship in my sophomore year at WFMY-TV, the CBS-affiliate, a Gannett station, in Greensboro, North Carolina. When my internship was over I just kept going to the station. I just kept right on going.

I remember the news director was named Rob Allman. He works for the Christian Broadcasting Network now. He was a snappy dresser—cuff links, tie, crisp shirt every day, crisp collar. I knew that I wanted to be a news director and my grandmother used to say, "Dress for the position you want, not for the position you have." So I started then. Even as an intern, I made sure that I had shirts and ties on every day, dressing for the position that I wanted. Finally, after a year and a half, they hired me as an overnight writer and on the assignment desk. I got the job because I impressed people. When they put the e-mail out that they hired me, people thought that I'd already been working there. I was just about to graduate and I was already working in the business and had my foot in the door.

I was a kid who didn't really know what he was doing at night, working the assignment desk by myself. I would hear something happening on the scanners and I would grab a camera and go shoot it. I'll never forget, after my first week the chief photographer said, "Listen, son, if you're going to go out and shoot I need to at least show you how to white balance." This was after a week of bringing back green and blue video from overnight.

I just wanted to do anything that needed to be done. I remember going to shoot some sports stuff with the sports guys because they didn't have anybody else to go and I'd say, "I'll go shoot it." You know, if I heard about something that needed to be done, I would go do it.

I was at that station for two years when a story was done in a publication of the National Association of Black Journalists exploring why there weren't more African-American producers in newsrooms. Most news directors in the story said they couldn't find them. The guy who wrote the article said that he knew of one and that he'd just graduated from college and had television experience. He put my name in the article and I started getting phone calls. I started getting phone calls from all over the place.

One of the calls I got was from WSVN-TV in Miami. In about a two month period of time I probably visited five or six stations. Here I am, a little kid from North Carolina who had never really been anywhere, never really travelling outside the state except for sports. I flew down to Miami and took the job at WSVN, which is known as one of the more dynamic, innovative breaking news stations in the country. I worked there for three years in a lot of different capacities. Then I got a call from Hearst Corporation and they offered me my first management job and I went to Cincinnati, Ohio, as the executive producer. I was there for two years, then went to WCNC-TV in Charlotte, North Carolina, a Belo station, as the news director. I was there during 9/11.

While I was in Charlotte, Hearst and Belo worked together to put together a producer academy. I worked on that task force and while working closely with the Hearst executives again I knew I wanted to come back and work for Hearst. So after Charlotte, I went down to WESH-TV in Orlando, Florida, where Bill Baumann[1] was the general manager. The news director at the time was a guy named Ed Trauschke, who had been a reporter for over twenty years in the Orlando market before becoming a news director. So we both were leaders of the newsroom with two different types of experiences. I brought the producer and executive producer experience and he brought the reporting experience. I was able to learn so much from him as a former reporter, listening to how he critiqued the reporters' packages and how he looked at the story structure. And he was able to learn from me as far as producing and showcasing, being what I call a "show doctor"—how to improve a newscast. This is what I would say is my strength—putting together a newscast and improving a newscast.

Where was your first job as news director?

My first full news director job was WDSU-TV in New Orleans. I got there about eight months before Hurricane Katrina hit. For me it was really baptism by water and fire. A lot of it was less about being a news director and more about being a leader. All the things I'd learned over the years from different news directors really played an important role, as well as a lot of things that

---

[1] Bill Baumann had previously been the news director at KCRA-TV in Sacramento.

were instilled in me by my family, by my grandmother, in terms of how you treat people and how you take care of your people. Do unto others as you want people to do unto you. I think those basic principles really helped us in that time. That's what that news director time was about—it was really about leadership.

During Katrina it was well documented about what happens when there's lack of leadership. We saw some great things happen because of people who saw the opportunities to be leaders and not run away from situations in times of crisis. As well as how you come out better than you were before the crisis.

I felt that we did a lot of good things during Hurricane Katrina, but I think the biggest thing we were able to accomplish was we were able to reinvent how we were distributing information. When the floodwaters eventually flooded our tower we kept right on producing news. We were online. Eventually we were broadcasting on DirecTV. Then we were getting on cable systems outside of New Orleans because most of the people had left the city. As a company we were trying to figure out how do we get our news product on the cable systems in the cities where these people are located. So in Houston and Mobile, Alabama, and Jackson, Mississippi, we were able to pump our signal into those markets to give information—good information— to the people who were in those markets who had been evacuated from New Orleans and couldn't come back home. Yes, we may not have been broadcasting in the city of New Orleans, but many would argue that it didn't matter because everybody had left the city, but then at that point you could find WDSU on DirecTV. So overnight we went from being a local television station to a regional network. That's what we called it, the WDSU Regional Network. This was the first time that had been done. Now when you look at DirecTV during any major hurricane or major weather event in a particular area you'll find local stations on there, and we were the first ones to work out a deal to be able to do that.

Talking about internships and how to get your foot in the door, you took an aggressive approach to your internship in that even though the internship was over, you didn't let it end for you.

I'm a big believer that you should be able to land a job from your internship. It may be a year after your internship, but you should have impressed every single person in that newsroom. Everybody has to know your name.

I say to interns, "You have to keep your foot in the door some kind of way—even when your internship is over." Just like basketball players in the NBA, when basketball season is over they don't stop playing basketball— they're somewhere practicing, they're playing pick-up games, they're working out. They're doing the things they need to do to stay in their profession. With interns and college kids I think it needs to be the same way.

There's always a PBS station that's looking for an intern or somebody to do some work for them. There's always a sports team that's looking for somebody to pick up a camera and do some things for them. There are non-profit organizations that are looking for people to make videos and make PSAs for them. I am interested not so much in the internships that people were doing, but what are you doing in your free time? How creative are you? That tells me whether somebody deserves to be in our industry and our profession when I'm looking at hiring. What else were you doing? Even if you go to a school that is not as well equipped and may not have all the tools and technology, there are still ways today with computer editing and affordable technology to do it on your own. I'm always asking, "Okay, what have you done with your time?" If you're a senior and you're in front of me and you have nothing to show for it, that tells me that you've wasted a couple years of school.

In my opinion, too many students wait too late in their time in college to do internships. Some even wait until after they've graduated to complete their internship.

Senior year is too late. You need to do your internship in your sophomore year because it's going to take a couple internships for you to learn what we do. How else are you going to be able to put something together to do some quality work? How else are you going to get your foot in the door?

I tell interns on their first day, "A lot of you are going to find out that you don't want to do this. And that's okay." This year we had an intern here for one day. The next day she sent us an e-mail that said, "You know what? I don't want to do this. This is not for me." So even if people figure out that this is not for them, I think that we have done our jobs as journalists. We should be giving interns an accurate reflection of what is going on, how we do our jobs and the importance of what we do.

The last few semesters we've had a lot of interns go on and find jobs in the industry. I know of five who are reporting right now and two that are shooting. That's great, and that's still a small percentage, but the other ones that don't, that means they weren't cut out for our industry anyway.

It's very tough to be in our industry so we at least want to make sure that the ones who come through KCRA are being given an opportunity to learn everything they can. That's what I like about all the people here—the photojournalists, the editors, the producers, the reporters—we're all engaged with these kids. The ones who love being here and love being around what we do, we know they're cut out for it. This is a crazy business and you have to be just as crazy as we are to survive it. You've got to thrive on it. Your adrenalin has to pump when you're out on breaking news or when your show starts changing at the last moment. I think we're doing a good job of giving kids a real life experience of what it's like to be a journalist in the year 2011. If some of them say, "This is not for me," I'd rather them say that now than a couple years down the line when they're out working with a photographer and they've got a bad attitude because it's not what they want to do.

And I know that in the future we'll be hiring back some of these kids that weren't here that long ago. One of the interns who was here was on a job interview and had to go and do a live shot—on her job interview she had to do a live shot in the six o'clock show! She texted me about that—and they hired her. That's how they're interviewing people today. She was prepared for that job because of the opportunities that we provided for her here at KCRA, going out with photographers, doing stand-ups, doing interviews.

Since everything is moving to the web, do you think that today you have to have a website so that you can show that you have an understanding of the Internet?

That's exactly what it does. The fact that you have your own website shows me that you have an understanding of how it works and that you're going to be able to post stories and post blogs. Recently I hired a producer right out of college, out of the University of Missouri, who came recommended to me by one of the Hearst vice-presidents who said, "This is one of the smartest kids I know." And yes, at the University of Missouri they run their own NBC station there, KOMU-TV. She sent me a link to her website that showed her work. It had all the shows she was producing, it had a blog, it talked about her mission and what she wanted to do, plus her philosophy and all her news experiences. The fact that she knew Twitter and Facebook and all the social networking, it was clear that she was light years ahead of everybody else—and smarter than me in a lot of ways. I wanted to take that chance of bringing somebody to our team, then teaching her something about producing. And that has worked out great for us.

In the current environment, if you don't have your own website where you're constantly updating your work, you're already behind. I go back home to North Carolina every year and visit schools, like Elon College in North Carolina, where students are going out and doing stories on a daily basis right there on campus, editing on their laptops and posting them right to their website. Their professor pulls up the students' websites and we watch their work and critique it right then and there. They send me links to their new work constantly and I continue to go to their websites and can see their work. And TV stations have been hiring these kids left and right.

These days very few people are sending out reels of their work on DVDs. This is how fast the technology is changing. In just a few years' time we've gone from sending out VHS to sending out DVDs to sending out links to websites. I'd say that the last couple of people I hired I watched their link from my smart phone, from my Droid phone, usually on the weekend sitting beside the pool. I've hired a meteorologist that way and I've hired two reporters that way. I see their work on my smart phone, and if I like it I call them up right then and there. So the times have changed.

I encourage everybody to register their name as a domain name. Buy your domain name so that you can own it for life because it is so valuable.

Absolutely. If you don't own your domain name right now by the time you get finished reading this chapter of the book you should be putting the book down and going to get your domain name. You don't want somebody else owning your name. No matter what product you're putting out there, you have to own your own name.

We have so many ways of trying to promote and present the news—Facebook, Twitter. We post our videos on the website. Newspapers are creating and posting videos onto their websites. Where do you see things heading?

You know, as much as things are moving to a common ground, I would say that television is just as strong as it has ever been. Think about it. TVs are getting bigger, clearer, *thinner*. Wherever there is competition between television and something else—whether it's television and your phone, television and the computer, television and your iPad—people choose television. Head-to-head, television is still the chosen one. That was proven on the night when it was announced that Osama Bin Laden had been killed. A lot of people found out the information from a smart phone or some type of e-mail alert or a text. But they came to TV. That was one of the largest viewing nights of this year. People came to television to see President Obama's address that night. They weren't watching the president's address on an iPad or a phone. They were watching it on television.

I always say that given the options, people will still watch television. I'm still putting my money on local TV news. I believe in what we are doing. I believe that there is room for everything to exist. The web did not put the TV out of business, just like the TV did not put the newspaper out of business. They may be struggling a little bit and they may be reinventing themselves, just as in TV we are reinventing ourselves. But I think there is enough room for all of us to coexist.

There will always be new things and we will be in all of those platforms. But none of those platforms will replace our core business. That's what the bottom line is. So I would say that television is still the parent of all of them and television allows them to exist.

JULIE AKINS: News Director, KOBI-TV, Medford, Oregon

Telling stories is a passion for Julie Akins. As well as helping others to become storytellers.

I was working with KCRA reporter Sharokina Shams and telling her about this book when she said, "You need to talk to Julie Akins. She was my first news director and I wouldn't be in the business now if it hadn't been for her." A few days later I was on the phone with Julie, who said:

"That's right. Sharokina was writing for the Modesto Bee and was hired as a part-time person to help out on the assignment desk. This was a while ago when we were just starting to update our website. I noticed her web updates were crisp and well written and always spot-on. I started talking about her work and she expressed interest in being an on-air reporter. She would come in weekends and help out. Her first story was on a Thanksgiving weekend. She said, 'Can I put a story together and if the producer says it's okay, can we air it?' I said, 'All right, go ahead.' So she did it and you see where she is today. So it can happen."

Julie is author of the book *Common Miracles: Gifts from a Grateful Universe* and is currently writing another book.

The first question I ask everybody, what got you interested in news?

As a kid it was the habit of my family to read the paper in the morning and watch the evening news together. I remember watching in the living room with my note pad and comparing my observations to what I was reading in the newspaper. I think they thought I'd get tired of it in an hour or two and want to run out and play, but I didn't! I didn't move from my spot for a couple of days. Then my mom said, "Okay, kid, you've gotta go back to school." But my dad said, "Why? This is a better civics lesson than she's going to get going to school."

When I was in high school I did a public service program for a little radio station in a small town called Sumner. I didn't get paid for it. Once a week I produced this program that was targeted toward people my age, you know, people in high school. I was seventeen. I got some exclusive interviews on that show and it was a pretty big deal. I even sold a couple of small pieces to KIRO, one of the big radio stations in Seattle. I was just totally hooked.

I went to Pierce College, it's a community college. Then I went to the University of Puget Sound in Tacoma, Washington. I did radio news for several more years, which paid my way through school. Then when I was in my early twenties someone said, "Hey, you know radio's dying. You've gotta get into TV. That's where it's at." So I did.

My first TV job was as an assignment editor at KMST [now KION-TV] in Monterey, California. I went on to become a producer, then an executive producer and did that for several years.

Then I got this crazy job in Tampa, Florida, working on an I-Team. I was going out and doing stories and producing long-form projects with an anchor. It gave me what I was really missing, which was this holistic understanding of how it all comes together.

Going out in the field and doing that on the I-Team, I really got a better idea of how things come together and how long it takes to do things. What takes a story from being a really nice little 1:10 cookie-cutter package to being something more. I started learning about the arc of a story. I got so into it that I left and wrote for a newspaper in Tampa for a while, and loved that experience as well. I really felt that I gained better "chops" as a journalist—not just as a producer and executive producer and a manager. I went back to my roots and understood why it is that what we do is so damn important.

Eventually I became a news director, first in Oregon and then Las Vegas and Fresno where I met Sharokina. I was in the field again in San Francisco at KRON 4 prior to coming back to Oregon. Each experience has helped me.

What do you think is your greatest strength as a news director?

I'm a storyteller. If I didn't get paid to be in storytelling I'd be standing on a street corner trying to get people to give me change for storytelling. If I'm not at work working with people who are telling stories, then I'm teaching a class about storytelling.

Without trying to sound cerebral, I think storytelling is just as much a part of being human as pounding a drum. I think it's incredibly powerful. It helps us to know we're not alone. It's powerful because it can effect positive change when you hear what other people are going through or what other people are accomplishing. I love watching young storytellers progress and get great at what they do.

When interns come through your newsroom doors, what do you stress to them?

I think internships are really valuable, depending on how they're used. It's harder for interns in larger or major market stations because they're just not going to have the opportunity to do any hands-on work. They're going to be helping on the phones, helping on the assignment desk, things like that. In a San Francisco newsroom you're just not going to give an intern a camera and tell them to go out and shoot something. It's not going to happen. Being an intern in an entry-level station offers a lot more opportunity.

When the interns come in here the first thing I say to them is, "Why do you want to do this? What motivates you? Do you want to report? Do you want to write? Do you want to produce? Where is your interest?"

Then I try to give some basic rudimentary skills so that when they leave their internship they know, "Hey, did I really like this or did I just think this looked cool? And if I really like it, this is the part that I like best." Then they can go back to school with a little more focus on their education.

I tell people who come in for internships, "Come in and act like it's a job. Show up on time. Be here when you say you're going to be here. Come dressed appropriately for work." I've learned over the years to assign teams. I'll assign an intern to a particular anchor-reporter and say, "You two are tied together now. So his success as an intern is based on your ability to help him be successful, and vice versa." That way they go out every day with that reporter, they go on the set when that anchor is anchoring, they help shoot things, they help write things, do research. They become a team together. I've noticed that the reporter-anchor who has the intern assigned to them is very invested in the success of that intern, because they feel it reflects on them as well. They form a bond and that creates a successful opportunity.

If I was an intern, once I got into a newsroom I would be shopping around. Whose work do I most appreciate in this place? Okay, I'm going to try to glom onto that person and become their intern, because it works.

KCRA reporter Sharokina Shams doing a live shot via the
webcam of her laptop. Sharokina was one of the journalists who
was given their break into TV news by news director Julie Akins.

I encourage students to get an internship as early as they can. I feel that students who wait until their senior year to do their internships is too late to get a taste for the job that they're studying for.

I would agree. The sooner the better. If they can get in during their sophomore or junior year and start rolling up their sleeves, it can be really terrific.

My own son, who has some interest in communications, came in and did a one-day practicum with me and by the end of it he said, "I could not possibly work in broadcasting. You boil everything down too far. I can't stretch my writing enough. It's too difficult to try and tell a story in twenty seconds." Now he's doing an internship at *The Oregonian* and he loves it. So the sooner you know whether this is or isn't for you, the better.

I've got a couple of reporters who've got their Masters Degrees because their undergrad education just didn't prepare them. They had to go into a masters program to get real hands-on experience. As you and I both know, that's really what it takes. Of course, you want to understand theory. Of course, you have to be informed. Of course, you have to understand how government works and have a general idea about courts. And how to write—boy, that's so urgent. But hands-on experience is really what makes the difference. Any way you can get that, the sooner you can get it, the better off you are.

When you're hiring someone who hasn't worked as a reporter before, what are you looking at?

Of course, they have to have a reel and resume, so like any news director I click on their link and look at the work they're doing. I'm scouting for potential. Is their delivery energetic? Do they know the difference between when they look good and when they don't look good? If the montage of all their various stand-ups and live shots is real or fake, because a lot of times in school they don't have a live truck. Is it still effective? If they're putting in shots that don't look good or don't communicate clearly, that's concerning. If they're rambling or their stories aren't interesting, another concern is raised. All that tells me that they're not yet objective enough about themselves to know when they look good and when they don't. That's not a deal-breaker, but it tells me how hard I'm going to have to work with that person. Are they an effective speaker? Is their voice appropriate to the story? Do they know how to communicate in a way that shows me a certain depth? Do they understand their story? Is it written well enough that it doesn't have gaping holes and leave me with big questions? Those are the things that I'm mostly looking at.

You know they're going to come in rough. There are going to be some speech things, some tracking things that we're going to have to work on. There are going to be some writing things. They're going to have to tighten their stories, because they always come with these visions of three-minute packages that just are not going to make air. We're going to have to work on how they're reporting live and being fluid in a live shot and being able to ad-lib. We're going to work on their shooting and editing. So I'm looking for raw material.

But if they don't have any judgment, that stops me from going farther with them. When I say judgment—if they have stories on their tape that are just bizarre, that don't make sense. Why would you put them on a tape? If that story is not interesting, if it doesn't have anything for the viewer to get involved in. If they do it poorly and just send it in and think it's okay, then what can I do with that?

How important is it for an applicant to have a website to blog and post their video stories to?

When I get a DVD and a resume in the mail I just go, "Ugh, come on. Really?" It doesn't mean that I won't look at it, and I have hired people off of DVDs, but it's so much more preferred to go to a website—and it doesn't have to be a polished website. I can take their resume and a link to their reel on Youtube, I can do it that way. But it tells me something if they have a website that has their resume and qualifications, their references, their resume reel with several different clips, plus some other longer-form pieces. And, because everybody's a multi-platform journalist now, if they have any kind of a blog that shows me how they work in social media, that definitely helps. It distinguishes yourself as opposed to sending an e-mail with a link or a hard copy of a DVD and a resume in the mail, because it's not that world anymore. If you want to look like you're ready to play in the world that currently exists, a website gives you a leg up.

I also think it's important to have a professional Facebook page, because people go online now and look at your Facebook as part of their hiring process. Keep your personal page locked and set up a professional Facebook page that has a good picture and shows your work.

If you're in college and producing packages or you're anchoring, take your best stuff and stick it on there, the way reporters here at KOBI post their best stuff on a professional Facebook page.

I wouldn't do the first year, though. Once you make a bad impression, you have a bad impression. A prospective employer might not go back and take a second look. But six months from graduation, when your work's good enough, create your professional Facebook page and start posting your best stuff there.

A lot of interns feel they have to put their reel together during their internship, then never touch it again. In today's digital world, there's no reason why they can't keep working on their reel after the internship's over, or even after they've graduated.

Absolutely. If you're interning at a large station, you're probably not going to be shooting your own tape and putting a piece together. It's just not happening. So I'll look at it and immediately go, "Wow, one of the photographers shot this and edited it for you." It's beautiful, but it's not going to tell me whether you can do that kind of work here. That actually is off-putting to me.

I need people who are multi-media journalists. This is their first job and they will be shooting and editing their own stuff. You have to show me what you can do. You have to show me stories that only you produced, shot, wrote, edited, voiced and fronted. I need to see that whole package. If you can't pick up a camera and go out and do a story at the station you're interning at, then you have to find another way to do it, either through your campus TV station or your local public access station. Every city has them. They have Final Cut Pro edit stations and pretty good gear. You can become a member for twenty bucks, grab a camera, go out and produce stories and put them on the air. You can stay informed in your local community, read the paper, watch the news, see what's going on, then go out and do stories, put them on your Facebook page and make a resume reel.

Every news director will want to see what you've done in the last six months. I don't need to see something that someone produced three years ago.

This is so much more important now with the shift in the industry to the one-person digital journalist.

Things have shifted and that's a fact. There are all kinds of discussions about whether that's a good thing or a bad thing. All I can say is it's a real thing. It's shifted to a point where reporters, certainly starting out and sometimes in very big markets, are shooting, writing and editing their own stories—everything on their own. Now, they don't set up their own live shots, we have a live truck operator. But other than that, they do the whole thing themselves. That's just the way it is. If you can't bring that skill set to the table, then you're not going to get the first job.

You have to see your camera the way a musician sees a guitar. This is your essential tool in order to express your art. You have to know how to use it effectively. Just the way you work on your writing—you need to work on your shooting and editing. You have to do it well. Otherwise, you can't get through the gate to your first job.

I was an MMJ at KRON-4 in San Francisco before I came back to be a news director again, and I loved it, so I know it can be done. You're also not as intrusive and people are more forthcoming. You just wander around, putting your little camera up there and saying, "Hey, what happened?" Oh my gosh, people just open right up. And it's not so formulaic like it can be when you've got the intimidation of a whole big crew.

Actually, it feels really great, driving out to your story, grabbing your camera and your tripod and your mic and getting out there and shooting on your own. It creates a lot of intimate moments as a journalist and can create great stories.

There's a beauty to working with a team member and talking through your story, but sometimes people see things differently. When you're a multimedia journalist it gets down to how *you* see it. If you don't get that shot, you can't write that line. But it's incumbent upon you to get those shots. You can't blame somebody else if the story's not good. It's all in your hands. You might as well embrace it and have fun with it.

When you go out on an interview, don't talk—listen. When you go out on a scene, don't worry about whether your shoes are going to get dirty or whether you're going to rip your skirt. Become involved in the story, think about what you're looking at, shoot it, edit it, put the story together and keep yourself out of the way. If you don't make it about you and keep it about the story, you'll do fine.

I think the thing is, don't do it if you don't love it. And make sure you keep yourself out of the way and put the story first. That's what's going to make you a good storyteller—keep the story first.

LILIAN KIM: Reporter, KGO-TV, San Francisco, California

One day in the early 1990s a young intern observed a story I was shooting with KCRA reporter Lisa Breckenridge, now with Fox News 11 in Los Angeles. The intern was Lilian Kim, another intern among the waves of interns who crash against the shores of TV newsrooms across the country, only to recede into dark waters, never to be seen again. Or so I thought.

During lunch. Lisa shared her insight with Lilian on writing, stand-ups and her resume. Later I shot a stand-up for Lilian and was impressed that she wrote it out and did it in one take, instead of trying to improvise it and stumbling over what she was going to say again and again.

A year later there was a buzz around the newsroom and Lisa said to me, "Hey, did you hear? Lilian's coming back."

I'd been in the business for a dozen years by then and Lilian was the first intern I could remember who'd actually gotten a job.

Lilian Kim wound up working at KCRA for five years before going on to CNN and is now a reporter with KGO-TV in San Francisco.

When did you first become interested in news?

Early on. I would watch the four o'clock news after Donahue and always thought what the news people did was cool. Plus, I loved current events.

I knew I wanted to pursue broadcast journalism when I was in high school. But when it came time for college applications I ended up applying to schools that didn't have journalism programs. I remember reading about how Peter

Jennings was a college dropout. Other people told me you didn't have to major in journalism to be a TV journalist, so I wasn't too worried about my college choices. I went to U.C. Davis and majored in sociology and communications. Since I didn't go to a school like the University of Missouri, where there's a strong, hands-on journalism program, I had to rely on internships to get things going. I started my internship in my junior year, first at one Sacramento station, then at KCRA.

Lilian Kim as a reporter at KCRA, writing on deadline in a satellite truck with photographer-editor Brian Fong.

What was it like the first time you came into the newsroom?

Intimidating. I'd never worked in an adult place before. I was twenty and I'd always had part-time minimum-wage type jobs, like at a restaurant or retail store, but I'd never worked in a white-collar, professional office building before. I remember being intimidated by seeing adults walking around in their suits and professional clothes. College kids' budgets don't really allow you to buy expensive clothes, so I did the best I could with the small budget I had. I would wear nice pants or a nice blouse or something, but it was definitely important to look professional and blend in.

I learned that I had to take the initiative. I had to make things happen. I couldn't just sit around and wait for people to give me opportunities—I had to make my own opportunities.

I figured this out after not really doing anything the first couple weeks I was there. I remember thinking, "This sucks. I don't want to just sit around, answering phones." Some interns will just sit around passively and not get anything out of it. I didn't want to do that.

So I'd ask, "Can I go out on a story? Can I shadow a reporter? Can I hang out with a photographer? Can I watch someone edit?" I had to be aggressive.

You spent a semester interning at one TV station, then for your second semester internship you applied to KCRA. Why?

I didn't think the first station was very receptive to helping interns. While I tried to make the most of it, I wanted to see if another station would be different—and it was *very* different. KCRA had a structured internship program and the people were much more willing to help a student. You could be an assignment desk intern, a special projects intern or a consumer reporter intern. The environment was more conducive to people who wanted to break into the business.

Did you approach this second internship with greater focus?

I was always focused. For me it was never even a question of "Would I be a reporter?" I knew I was going to be a reporter.

My first priority was to do my internship well, because that was why I was there. My second priority was to make a resume tape.

KCRA reporter Lilian Kim working with photographer Mike Orcutt on couples tying the knot on Valentine's Day.

Most of my internship hours were devoted to helping the special projects producer I was assigned to, so for making my tape, I worked on it either when I had some down time during my internship hours or on my own time. That was what was great about KCRA—they allowed interns to use the equipment and resources once you were "off the clock." I befriended a couple photographers and they were kind enough to help edit my stories for me.

I would come in on my days off, after my internship day was over-- whatever hours I had to in order to work with the photographer who was helping me.

You have to show people that you're determined, because no one wants to help someone who isn't serious. You have to show that you're sincere and have a strong interest in the business. And you have to be nice. Now that I'm a reporter helping out interns, I find an intern's personality goes a long way. If you like them, you want to help them out.

What did you discover about the actual work of putting a TV story together?
That it takes a lot of time. I was surprised to see how much ended up on the cutting room floor. It's a lot of work to put that minute-thirty together.

It was hard to take all the information you had and make it into a cohesive 1:30 story. That's very hard to do. As a beginner you think every element is important so you want to include everything.

What did you have on your resume tape?
I wanted visual stories. I wanted something that not all the other interns had. Bill Bauman, the news director at the time, said to me, "Don't put the story of when the President comes to town. Everybody does that kind of thing." I wanted an undated tape—because I didn't know how long my tape was going to last before I got a job.

Once you had your tape, what did you start doing?
I started mailing it out across the country. I sent them everywhere. Some were stations that I knew didn't have an opening, but I sent them a tape anyway simply because they were close to home, mostly small-market stations in California. Others I found through ads in trade magazines. It was different then because you had ¾" tapes that you had to mail. Now it's all gone to the internet. People just e-mail a link to Youtube. It's so different now.

I sent out thirty tapes and got six calls back. I took a job in Louisiana because I didn't have to shoot my own stuff.

If you were starting out today you'd probably have to be a one-man journalist.
But it's so different now—the cameras are a lot smaller, so it's much more doable.

You get your first job in Louisiana, more than halfway across the country. Was that hard for you?
No, I was eager to start my career. I remember my boyfriend and I having to break up before I left. At the time, my career was my first priority so I had no problem ending the relationship.

A lot of interns think they can find their first job close to home and that is so unrealistic. Even if you can find one in the same state, you're lucky—

unless, of course, you're from a small-market town. Getting that first job is really hard. You have to be prepared to move out of state.

Did you have to hit the ground running or did you have a training period?

I hit the ground running. I didn't know how to edit but I learned very quickly. I think that's the best way to learn. Just go in there and do it.

How long were you in Louisiana?

Six months. I went there thinking it would be two years because I signed a two-year contract. But then there was a change in ownership and the new managers decided to do away with contracts. Coincidentally, Bill Bauman, the news director at KCRA, called to tell me he wanted to start a reporter-trainee program and asked if I was interested. About a month later, I left the Louisiana station to go back to KCRA. It came at just the right time. I was very lucky.

What was it like coming back to the station where you'd been a student?

It was great because I loved KCRA. I loved the people. I'd learned so much there. It was like coming home. Looking back, I don't know if that was the smartest thing to do. It was difficult growing and learning in a top-twenty market where the quality is so much higher than where I was as a reporter. I had my embarrassing moments and made a lot of mistakes on the air. It's better to make those mistakes in a smaller market where it's expected. Having said that, I found that the staff was extremely patient and generous with me. The veteran journalists could have said, "Why do I have to work alongside someone who has zero experience?" But, amazingly, everybody was so nice.

Now you're working in the Bay Area, where KRON in San Francisco has been using MMJs since 1999. Is this happening in other stations?

Yes, KPIX is doing it. Some of their photographers have added reporting to their duties and some reporters are now shooting their own material. KGO started training a handful of reporters last year. KNTV started recently, as well.

I'm scheduled for training next year. I'm actually looking forward to it. I want the added skill.

There's no denying that this is the direction the industry is going. There's no point in fighting it because the technology is making it happen.

Final thoughts?

I got my job at KCRA because I apparently made a good impression during my internship. Approach your internship like a job. You never know where those relationships are going to take you in the future.

TRACY BRYAN: Former Reporter, KCRA-TV, Sacramento, California

Tracy Bryan is living proof that there can be life after news. When Tracy decided to shift her focus from being a reporter at KCRA-TV to starting a family, she walked away from the newsroom to apply her media knowledge to raising donor transplant awareness. Tracy is currently Director of Public Relations for Golden State Donor Services and is the president of Donate Life California a non-profit organ tissue donor transplant organization.

What attracted you to news?

I went to the University of Oklahoma in the mid-1970s. I originally was going to be a Spanish major, but I quickly realized that wasn't such a great idea because there were millions of people who could speak Spanish better than I ever could. So I kind of fell into Journalism because I love to write. I love Hemingway and the simplicity of his prose, his broad-brush look at the world. I found that broadcast journalism writing for radio and TV was in that broad stroke, big picture style. You didn't have to get down and dirty with the details like you do in newspaper writing.

I did an internship at a radio station in Oklahoma City where they let interns be on the air, so I was on the air for the first time, doing a story. And that was thrilling. One of the DJ's was a mentor to me and said, "Get your foot in the door any way you can. Get into a smaller station, you'll learn a lot"—which is true.

Did any of your journalism classes prepare you for writing for radio?

I don't think I really understood broadcasting until I went to work for my first radio station at KNOR in Norman, Oklahoma. It was a talk radio station. Nancy Kolb was the news director and she totally knew how to write news and how it was done. I still remember the first day I worked there, I was handwriting my story and Nancy said, "No. You have to write on the typewriter." This was back when we still had typewriters. "You have to type your story. You cannot ever use longhand. That's ridiculous, there's not time. You have to really go fast." She also expected us to be on-call 24/7, which I didn't understand. I thought I'd go to work and then I'm off. "No, no, no. You're on all the time. If there's a breaking news story, you're on." That was a good lesson for me.

Tracy Bryan with co-anchor Chris Wilson on news set at KNAZ-TV in Flagstaff, Arizona.

But I really wanted to be in TV, so I took my radio script and went to a place that would videotape me at a table reading the news. I read the news in front of a camera and had it taped, then KNAZ in Flagstaff, Arizona, hired me. They were the 202nd market station out of 204 markets in the nation. Then when I got there the news director who'd hired me had left and I was told, "Well, you can still have the job if you want it." So I took it, and I was the anchor, reporter, producer and assignment editor, and janitor. That's where I learned that out of all of the jobs, my favorite was reporting—

because you're out in the field, in the front row seat of life, talking to people, and it was interesting.

That job lasted six months, then my long-time boyfriend from college asked me to marry him and I moved back to Oklahoma. I was going back to the 35th sized market from the 202nd. That's quite a leap—and it was difficult. I took a job in public relations for a year, then the Oklahoma oil boom went bust and I was laid off.

I turned to my DJ radio mentor, who advised me, "If you want to be in TV, you're not getting any younger. You need to pick the station you want to work for and don't leave until the news director sees you. Just sit there and wait until they talk to you—because they're not going to give you an interview. Just go in there and say, 'I'm not leaving until you talk to me.'" And that's what I did.

I chose KWTV because it was the number one station and it had a position open. It wasn't for a reporter but a production assistant, which was basically a gofer, but it occasionally allowed you to do morning cut-ins, which sounded good to me. I went in at 8 o'clock in the morning and told the receptionist, "I want to see the news director." She said, "He's busy all day. Do you have an appointment?" I said, "No, I don't. But I'm going to sit here until he has a minute. I want to talk to him."

So I sat out there and at one o'clock the news director came out and said, "I understand you want to see me and you're not leaving until you do." I said, "That's right." Then he said, "I want you to know that I'm skipping my lunch to do this and I haven't eaten anything all day. But you can have five minutes because I just want to get rid of you." So we went back to the newsroom and I showed him a few minutes of my tape and he was not impressed. He asked me one or two questions and then said, "Bye bye."

I realized that I was not going to be getting a job, so I thought, "What can I do to change his negative outlook of me? What would appeal to him?" He was a big guy. I don't know how much he weighed, but I bet he hadn't missed many lunches. So I decided I'd buy him lunch. I went to Kentucky Fried Chicken, got a big old meal deal, took it back to the receptionist and said, "Can you give it to him with this note?" And the note said, "Thanks for skipping lunch. I hope in the end it will be worth it for both of us."

He called me that night and said, "I want you to know that two other people were much more qualified for this position. But you obviously know how to get people to talk to you. You have perseverance and you use your creativity to get results. So you've got the job."

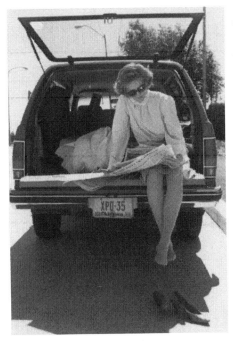

"The life of a reporter—hurry up and wait." Tracy Bryan during reporting days at KWTV in Oklahoma City.

How long did it take for you to move up to reporter?

It took me a year and it was a great year, I learned a lot. I wrote VO-SOTs, got to do the morning cut-ins. Then around six months into it there was a big explosion at one of the oil refineries, it was around noontime, all the reporters were out. They said, "Tracy, go out there and do the reports and you're going to be live!" And I still remember, they took me live and luckily the shot was only a head shot because my knees were knocking so hard I thought I was going to fall down, I was so scared. After my first live shot they realized that I actually could report and they started sending me out every time they were short a reporter, even though I wasn't being paid as a reporter.

You've seen lots of interns come and go through newsrooms over the years. What is your advice to them?

My advice is not to do an internship at a big station because you spend most of your time answering phones and not really learning anything. If you go to a smaller market you're much more apt to be used because they're short-staffed and don't have resources. You'll get a lot more experience and be able to jump in there.

You need to do an internship early to see if that's what you want to do. People think news is a glamorous vocation, but they only see the end product. They don't see all the work that goes into it and what it takes to get people to talk to you. You're out in the elements, dealing with deadlines and stress. It's crazy.

My big piece of advice for people trying to get their foot in the door is to start at the bottom. Persevere. Don't give up. And be creative.

I chose to get out of it when I decided to have a family. I did not want to have those kinds of hours and try to raise a child. There are definitely sacrifices you have to make if you want to do news and I wasn't willing to work 24/7 and be on-call and not be able to be with my child when I needed to.

KCRA reporter Tracy Bryan outside the Governor's Mansion in Little Rock, Arkansas, on November 3, 1992, the night Bill Clinton won the Presidency. With KCRA chief photographer Mike Rhinehart.

Did being in TV news and having a public face in the community help you get into your next career?

Yes, definitely. There was a perception, and I believe it's true, that I have contacts that are useful. I mean, if you stay in the same community where you were as a reporter, then you have contacts both within the community and with the media.

And I know what a story is. It's astounding to me that people in public relations have no idea what makes a news story. I know how to sell a story to a TV station to get them to show up.

If you were still in the business, or just starting out, and you had to shoot and edit your own stories with a camcorder and a laptop, what would your reaction be?

I think I would actually like it. When I worked in Las Vegas for a short stint in 1988, we edited our own pieces and I *loved* having that creative control. Instead of me having to communicate with the photographer—and hoping that he or she "got" it—about what video I was writing to, I could actually make it happen myself.

I think writing shooting, editing, producing the story in my mind would have been a dream come true. I would love to have had total control over the finished product. However, I know there's no way my stories would have been nearly as well-shot as they were, as I'm a writer first and a visual person second. So I definitely think something would have been lost in the mix.

I also think with the way the deadlines are today with multiple news shows and doing different versions of stories for each show, that this would be a mammoth amount of work. The deadlines we faced were almost insurmountable—even with a photographer working with me. So I think having to be everything would add to the overall stress. But, it might be fun. And I'd have died trying!

RICHARD SHARP: Reporter, KCRA-TV, Sacramento, California

Richard Sharp is another person who interned at KCRA, then embarked on his journey in broadcasting, and with whom I now work alongside as a colleague. For Richard, not only was his first TV news job as a reporter-photographer, his first *three* stations required him to report and also shoot his own stories. Richard is a tireless individual, which is a necessary character-trait because all of the roads he's taken in his career path have been the ones less-traveled.

What first made you interested in journalism?

When I was a teenager some people said I had a deep voice and that I should be a broadcaster. I was floored that someone said it was something I would be good at. At the time I couldn't really read or write very well and it seemed like something that was so far from what I could achieve. However, the more I learned about it, the more interested I became. It sounded like a fun job, running around, hearing about people's stories and learning more about the world.

I went to the University of Utah and got a Broadcast Journalism and Communications degree. While in college, I was a radio board operator for a couple of commercial music stations and that was fun.

When I was finishing up school I saw a couple job postings around the college for an evening producer at a small UHF TV station that only broadcast to Park City, Utah, about 45 minutes away. It was something like a ski channel during the winter, so a lot of it was Olympic stuff and ski resort types of reports. I applied and went in for an interview. They saw that I was eager—and *inexpensive*—end of story. I don't think it had much to do with talent. But I'd like to think it did.

I anchored and reported for a half-hour evening show every day of the week. I'd go to school in the morning, then race up to Park City to be there by noon, and then usually stayed until nine or ten at night. Do all the work on the show, then hustle home and do it all again the next day.

We'd go out and talk to a lot of athletes and film community happenings. I did stories at the police department, did stories with cancer patients who were having benefits and other stuff.

I think it paid $200 a month for all of that work. I didn't do it that long, but I got the experience that I needed out of it. I got an understanding of how much work this industry requires of you on a daily basis.

In your broadcasting major, how well did your classes prepare you for a career in broadcasting?

Fundamentally, I don't think it prepares you very well for deadlines. It prepares you for how to be a good writer. It prepares you for how to be a good journalist. It prepares you for how to gather elements. In college we had a couple days or a week to do a story. But it doesn't tell you how to do it in one hour or two hours or eight hours, if you have the luxury of being able to do that every day. That was the hardest learning curve. Everything you learn in college goes out the window when you're told to go do it in a couple hours' time. That's, I think, what they don't prepare you for enough. Also, in college you receive a tremendous amount of guidance, whereas in my first job they just gave me the gear and said, "Go cover these stories."

You also did an internship at KCRA.

Yes, I interned at KCRA during the summer of 1997. I applied to internships all over the country because I wanted to see what media was like outside of Utah. I got accepted into many different stations, but most of them restricted interns to staying in the newsroom and answering phones. The KCRA internship was on weekends and I figured that on the weekends I'd have a better opportunity to get out and work more closely with the reporters and photographers. Sure enough, that's exactly what happened. I worked as an intern from 6 AM to 6 PM. Put in as many hours as I could. It was an eye-opening experience to see how a major operation in the 19th market treated news. KCRA has such an incredible reputation. After that I always wanted to get back there.

I graduated in March 1998, but I started looking around long before then. I knew how long it could take to get a job in this business. I sent out 150 resume tapes all across the country. I got a couple callbacks, but Greenville, Mississippi, market 180, was the only job offer. The interview was all done over the phone. Two weeks after graduation I took the job sight unseen. Packed up all my belongings, drove out there and signed a piece of paper. At the time I thought everybody did this, but looking back it was a tremendous amount of trust. I was moving to the middle of the Mississippi Delta, basically 180 degrees from what I was used to, growing up in the West. It was an anchor-reporter position on paper, but it was much more than that in reality. For an anchor-reporter position in the 180th market I was making $16,500 and for the work I did I would assume that was a steal.

My first story was a murder where a woman had a restraining order on a guy, the guy came close to her and she stabbed him in the chest with a 12-inch steak knife. Stabbed him so hard it bent the knife at the hilt. I'd never covered a murder before. I'd never covered anything like that. I showed up at the police department in this small town and the police chief says, "You want to talk to me?" I said, "Yeah, sure!" On the way in I noticed two women crying outside his office—and one of them happened to be the woman who'd stabbed the man. Never having ever been in that situation before, I said, "Is this the woman?" And she nodded yes. I knew nothing about sensitivity and said, "Can I talk to you on camera?" She said, "No, but you can talk to my sister." So I said, "Okay, I'll be right back."

I go into the police chief's office and he says, "You want to see the murder weapon?" Again, not knowing anything, I say, "Sure." I'm thinking CSI plastic bag, everything nicely contained. He pulls out a manila envelope and takes out the steak knife with blood encrusted on it from when the woman stabbed the guy—and plops it down on his desk. I was filming it with the camera, looking through the viewfinder and zooming in on all the blood droplets and everything. Man, I almost threw up. The sheriff knew I was green and just had a big old smile on his face. It was an eye-opening experience.

After I finished with the interview I spoke with the suspect's sister. She took me to the house to show me the blood trail. I'm filming the blood trail inside the murdered guy's house in the middle of Mississippi. Three days into the job I'm thinking to myself, "What on earth am I doing?"

At the same time it was wildly exciting! It was so vastly different from anything I'd ever done before. It was addicting.

KCRA reporter Richard Sharp logging and writing on deadline in a live truck in the field.

I would come in on weekends at 7 AM and have to be my own assignment editor, my own photographer and my own reporter. I generally put 200 miles on the car shooting four to five, sometimes as many as six different stories. I'd package one and do VO-SOTs on the rest. Then I'd produce the entire half-hour newscast, write the show and edit the show from all of the stuff I'd shot and all of the news feeds. I'd get all the tapes in order for the technical crew, tape the scripts together for the teleprompter, then go out and anchor the show, which was a half an hour newscast at 10 o'clock. Just a tremendous amount of work. Looking back I can't believe I was ever able to do that much. But you're hungry. You want to do it. You're not focused on talent. You're focused on getting the job done.

I was in Mississippi for just over a year, then moved to west Texas for a year. In Texas they had some photographers, but many times I would shoot on my own. Then I moved to Toledo, Ohio, which was market 60, for almost two years. Toledo was the same thing. Many times the photographer would be setting up the live truck and I would be shooting.

Eventually the situation arose to report for KCRA and I jumped on it. I never thought I'd be able to work here, but here I am. Been here for seven years now.

When you got your first job, did you expect that you'd have to be your own cameraman as well as reporting?

Yes, I did. At the time, I think that was expected in all the smaller markets. The first machine I shot on was a ¾" umbilical cord deck and I edited on ¾", which is ancient now. It was hard to do. People often say, "Wow, can't wait 'till I don't have to shoot." But it made me a better person. I learned so much from shooting my own stuff. It made me a better journalist. It taught me that storytelling is more than just writing. It made me understand how to get things on the air in a more efficient manner. I think now more than ever, that's especially the case with digital media. Easier, quicker, faster, better. And I'm still learning, like when I shoot my own stuff on the Android. It's still a learning experience and still very fun to do.

How many interns do you think have an accurate sense for what this business is?

I would say less than 5%. Most interns have no idea what they're getting into. Sometimes I'll even discourage them because I don't think they're ready, or I don't think they understand what it's going to take. Many just grossly misunderstand what this job is going to require of your life. It's very exciting, but it's also very taxing. If you're not up for it, stay out.

I often think about which I would rather have colleges do: prepare students for the intense deadlines of the real world or give them a good, basic foundation of what journalism is, which is the writing and understanding the decisions you're going to have to make in the field. Every single time I come back to thinking that colleges that teach the basic fundamentals of journalism are far and away the most important. You have a lifetime to learn the deadlines, and deadlines are always changing. I would rather have someone come out of college who knows the basics of journalism and makes good decisions, because you can build on that once they get out into the field.

You've been a one-man journalist in your first couple of jobs—do you see yourself having to shoot your own camera again somewhere down the road?

I think it's inevitable. The electronic media and the ease of getting video from the field is so powerful that I think every person who is a journalist will have to do it in some way, shape or form. I fully expect to be doing it again.

Ashleigh Walters stands by with a camera, waiting for Governor Mark Sanford to exit his office at the State House after it came out that he had a mistress in Argentina.

ASHLEIGH WALTERS: MMJ, WPTV-TV, West Palm Beach, Florida

Ashleigh Walters' parents "have always been news junkies" and at an early age Ashleigh hopped on board. She studied at the University of Colorado at Boulder, majoring in Broadcast News journalism, and also received a second degree in Fine Arts with an emphasis in painting and a minor in Business Administration.

Ashleigh started her television career on a magazine-style show in Denver, Colorado's KUSA-TV, producing and interviewing guests and several celebrities. It was not long until she made the switch to news as an anchor and multi-media reporter in 2008 at WLTX-TV, covering the political and education beats in Columbia, South Carolina, the state capitol. We spoke in July 2011, shortly after she had moved to West Palm Beach, Florida, to work at WPTV in her next step up the news ladder as an MMJ.

Her journalism journey can be followed at her website ashleighwalters.com, which she maintains herself.

What got you interested in news?

My parents always had the television on local and national news. Every morning before school there were at least three newspapers on the table to read. Then in about eighth grade, I took a journalism class and it just went from there. I always knew my career would be in journalism because the day-to-day challenge is never the same twice.

When you were in college and you had your sights set on getting into TV news, were you interested in solely being a reporter or did you see that being a reporter-photographer was something you were going to have to do?

In school I enjoyed shooting and editing the stories, thinking that, "This is my project. I made this happen." The cameras in school were Sony and Panasonic and were very similar to what I'm using as an MMJ today. They had the functions for manual white balance and focus, as well as the automatic settings for the people who were less comfortable.

I realized that knowing what it takes to make things happen behind the scenes makes you a better reporter and vice-versa. This goes for not only being multi-talented in the field, but also being well-versed in various parts of the news station. I think that if you can cross-pollenate in the newsroom and understand each others' jobs it's amazing how much better we all function.

I had an internship at KUSA-TV in Denver, which has been the number one station there for more than three decades. It was, by far, my best learning experience in college. When I heard that KUSA had the most competitive internship, that was the one I wanted. I told them I was interested in investigative journalism and they put me into the investigative unit with Paula Woodward, who is an exceptional reporter and has worked on some of the biggest stories in the Denver area. I worked with Paula and the rest of the Investigative Team and newsroom for two semesters, which was rare if not unprecedented at that station. I researched stories and was sent on undercover work with a hidden camera. School prepares you for the style of writing that you'll have to do and how to shoot, write, edit and produce a show, but there is nothing that prepares you like real world experience. There are so many things that you just have to learn by doing.

Ashleigh catches a hawk on her arm while anchoring the morning news at WLTX-TV in Columbia, South Carolina.

For example, one night they called me at home and said, "There's a fire up in Boulder County and we don't have anybody who can be there for the next hour and a half." And I said, "I'll go and I'll call you with the updates." So I went up to the control area around the wildfires and phoned back the breaking details. Volunteering to work in complicated and sometimes challenging situations, and proving that you can and will work hard and deliver, I think that's how you end up with the best experience.

I think with females in this profession, especially on the younger side of things, internships are where it weeds people out. A lot of interns say, "I only want to be an anchor." You can't get to that level without getting your hands dirty and proving yourself, and many anchors in today's newsrooms are asked to shoot, edit and write too.

There was a wonderfully talented friend of mine in journalism school who was beautiful, smart, had a great voice and presence. A reporter came from CNN and we all shot look-live's and were critiqued in front of the class. The reporter was tough on her, as he was critical of everyone. He challenged her, saying, "You're doing this wrong. . . . You have to change that." She turned to me, right then, and said, "I'm done. I can't do this. I can't handle this." If you can't handle criticism, and sometimes harsh criticism, then you won't last. However, if you can take a critique and make it work to your advantage, you'll learn and grow.

How did you get your first job?

It's kind of untraditional. I did have a tape and the paper resume as well, but they were not my key to my first job. I graduated college and spent the summer actively volunteering at the investigative unit at KUSA. I just wanted to be there. Then Paula Woodward, who had become my mentor, told me that a new magazine-style show was going to be starting up with an opening for a

ASHLEIGH WALTERS

production assistant. I interviewed and was hired as a fifteen-hour-a-week production assistant making about what you'd make as a hostess at a restaurant. I said, "I have a fine arts background. Can I do a five minute segment on some arts thing?" And they gave me that. I got to be on the air that first week. A month or two later, an interview with actor Kevin Bacon had been set up and nobody else could do it, and I made myself available. So, for my first professional interview out of college I interviewed Kevin Bacon. I continued to push myself and push my boundaries, asking, "Can I fill in as a host on the show?" "Yes." "Can I produce that and can I set up the interviews? Can I write that?" "Yes, yes and yes." Within a matter of months I was hired as a full-time producer, on-air interviewer and feature host on the show. I approached each day as, "There's no job too big or too small." Whatever they needed. I worked my way up the ladder.

I worked on that show for three years and I grew up a lot professionally in that time. But it just kept nagging at me that I wasn't doing the news.

Then the news department hired their first full-fledged MMJ. She'd been recruited because they couldn't believe that she could shoot and edit her own story and run it on the news on the same day. She spent the first weeks proving that she could edit and another couple of weeks proving that she knew how to shoot. In that market, where the photojournalism is really remarkable and sets a standard, she had to prove herself to other photojournalists until they respected her work. She earned it. I shadowed her a few times on my own time because I wanted to know what it was about.

I realized that the television journalism business was going towards the multi-media platform and that's where I wanted to be. KUSA is a Gannett station and they had some MMJ training coming up in Washington D.C. and I was accepted into the program. For a week I trained to become a "backpack journalist." Then they helped me to get hired by another Gannett station in Columbia, South Carolina—and I went! I took a pay cut to go become an MMJ!

What was it like when you came in the door at that first reporting job?

My first day, I was trained for how to post stories to the web because that was becoming so incredibly important—that we go to the web first before we go on-air with stories. Then on my first day shooting they handed me the camera, I didn't even have the chance to take it out of the bag and try it before I was sent to shoot a VO/SOT, and from there I was sent across town to shoot the top story, which I ended up having to turn into two packages. Then that night we had another top story break and I was sent for that. I think it ended up being an eighteen hour day. It was exhausting and difficult, but I was incredibly energized and excited. I think it was a very untraditional first day, jumping into the deep end. But I think that's really how it has to work.

I wound up proving myself pretty quickly. While tough, it was a tremendous opportunity because I became aware of my potential and my capabilities.

At your first station, were there only MMJs on the staff?

No, there was a blend of both, but there was definitely a push to get everybody up to speed. I remember the general manager saying that he never wanted to hire another person who couldn't shoot and edit, because the abilities had become vital to the success of our news environment.

There are times when having a photographer with you becomes tremendously valuable, and it is so much easier to work the story that way than having to do it all yourself. And sometimes the story result is better when you work as a team. Not every situation is perfectly structured to do it alone.

For example, while covering Governor Mark Sanford's battle against the stimulus, his affair with a woman from Argentina, and subsequent impeachment hearings, I was live at the State House every day. I would always bring my gear with me because there were so many instances where my photographer would be setting up the live truck and I'd need to go and get one more interview and edit it myself. And because of my skills, my photographer and I, as a team, were able to do better work.

Most people imagine that a reporter-photographer would be covering the visually-oriented stories, yet you wound up with the least visual beat there is.

That was an interesting challenge! When you're trying to be a storyteller and you're covering the legislature and politics, you have to think, "Well, there's nothing to show, but I have to find *something* to show. If it's a stack of papers that's the budget, how can I tell this story in a creative way? I ended up shooting the State House in so many creative ways that I could probably paint it from memory.

I was in Columbia for three years. Then, after getting my website up, word started to spread about my work and four different broadcast companies, each with multiple stations, approached me. Through that process I heard about WPTV in West Palm Beach and they'd heard about me and we started talking. I discovered it was a great station with a solid foundation and a good fit for my next step.

Do you call yourself an MMJ or backpack journalist?

Now I call myself a "Multi-Media Journalist" because that's what they call me. It's a title that keeps changing. I've heard MMJ, BPJ, and One-Man Band. MMJ seems to be the one that's sticking. And it does seem to be the perfect title because the Internet has become so much a part of the business.

Not only that, there's also the cell phone. People today often call it, "The Three Screens"—the TV, the computer screen and the smart phone. You have to get out "text alerts" and update the station's app while posting to the web and social media. You know, you want to have that beautiful package at six o'clock, but people have come to expect the flow of information to be fast, available and accessible.

At all times, when you're moving through your day, you have to be thinking about all the platforms: you show up on a scene, you're not only shooting video and an interview and trying to relay it back to the producers and the web team, but you're also shooting video and photos on your cell phone, and writing a story on your cell phone to text message back. It's just constant. You're writing the package in your head. You're making sure you have all the visual elements. Throughout your whole day you're thinking about the product on a broad scale.

That's part of the burden of thought while using social media to cover news, because I'm expected to be tweeting about what I'm doing and updating information that I've just learned about a story, potentially giving away the exclusive bits of my package which will air at six PM tonight—and I don't want the competition to go find that great interview that I just had.

As an MMJ, do you do as many live shots as a reporter who's teamed with a photographer or do you do more look-live's and FTP them in?

At my station now in West Palm Beach we are committed to doing constant live shots. I've been going live a lot more than in my past work. I also FTP look-lives and we're required to shoot our own stand-up teases.

Just yesterday two women were watching me as I worked alone to shoot a stand-up in multiple parts and they said, "We had no idea that one person would be doing all that." And the viewers really should never see the difference. It's like a little magic act.

What is your gear situation like?

I have a camera with a light on it and a tripod. I like to have a full light kit. I made the commitment with my last job to carry that huge thing everywhere with me. I have a stick mic with a cable and a wireless cube transmitter and a wireless lavelier microphone. Then, of course, rain gear for the camera because in Florida it rains frequently. And for my news car here, as in South Carolina, I'm driving a Toyota Prius. Everything I'm using is kind of toy size!

As a woman, do you have any particular perspectives on the business and the job?

Different women approach this job in a unique way. Many of my friends in the industry say, "I can't wait for when I can put down the camera and not have to do this anymore." I hear that all the time, and I think people are surprised when they realize that I am one who doesn't want to put it down.

Not every woman likes to sweat and hoist a huge, heavy tripod and camera through 110 degree heat and come back and try to fix their make-up and go on camera. It's not glamorous. I think many people assume it will be.

It's also an interesting thing trying to prove yourself as a photographer to your male peers. And it's fun to earn their respect. People assume, and sometimes rightfully so, that a woman is not strong enough to carry all that heavy gear and do all of it by herself. But I enjoy proving them wrong.

Where do you see yourself going in your future?

It's very hard for me to imagine doing this job and not having my hands on many parts of the puzzle. I would like to always be able to shoot and edit, even if I'm working on a team,

Ashleigh with her award for "Reporter of the Year" from the South Carolina Broadcaster Association in 2009 after her first year of television news reporting.

because it helps me tell the story in my own way. I could see myself down the road working on longer format television in some way, for a Discovery or Travel Channel. There's also something really beautiful about local news and the fast-moving nature, as you get to know a community in-depth.

You discussed the wage-cut when you got your first job—is there a financial sacrifice that you have to make when starting out in this business?

It is a sacrifice. I know from watching my friends who graduated at the same time as I did, but into different fields, that their earning power shifted immediately beyond mine. That can be frustrating. But they're often envious of how passionate I am for my work. That's the payoff. If you love to do the work, you're paid back tenfold in satisfaction from what you're not earning in salary.

I once passed by a video store and it had an advertisement for a video store manager and the salary that was posted was $3,000 more than I was making. But then, that store is probably out of business by now and I still have a job—and loving it.

CHRIS FRANK: MMJ, KAKE-TV, Wichita, Kansas

I think it would be fair to say that there are few one-man journalists whose roots can trace their career back not only to before the age of digital, but also before the age of video tape. Chris Frank of KAKE-TV in Wichita, Kansas, got his start with a spring-wound 16mm Bolex film camera.

When I embarked on this book I decided to go back to my roots to Wichita, Kansas, where there had always been reporter-photographers, referred to there as a "one-man band." The most notable was Larry Hatteberg at KAKE-TV, who had twice received the N.P.P.A. (National Press Photographers Association) Ernie Crisp Award as National TV News Photographer of the Year. Another

Holding a rare albino tiger at a private menagerie in Kansas.

KAKE reporter-photographer who I used to see on the streets, although never got to know until this interview, was Chris Frank, who'd been covering news in Wichita for a few years before I got there. Chris had been shooting his own news stories before he arrived in Wichita and, when given the opportunity to work as a traditional reporter working with a photographer, preferred to keep working on his own—three decades ahead of the trend in today's journalism.

When did you first get interested in news?

I grew up in Ponca City, Oklahoma, at a time when you only had the three major networks. As a family we watched Oklahoma City news, Tulsa, and occasionally Wichita stations. I was also a paperboy for the Ponca City News and that gave me an interest in reading headlines. I'd ask my dad questions like, "Why are guerillas fighting?" He would explain, "That's guerilla warfare." I think there was something that rubbed off, even if it was only the ink from the newspapers, but it gave me an interest in journalism. Then in English classes in high school I found a release in writing. And I had an older brother who worked at the local Ponca City radio station as a DJ, that also got me interested in broadcasting.

I first went to Northern Oklahoma College, a two year college in Tonkawa, then to Oklahoma State University in Stillwater, in the Radio-TV-Film department with an emphasis on 'News and Public Affairs,' which was broadcast journalism. I was doing news work on the two campus FM radio stations, one a low-powered pop-rock station covering the Stillwater and OSU campus, the other a high-powered NPR affiliate.

My break came during my senior year with a paid internship at the Tulsa ABC affiliate KTUL-TV. I drove to Tulsa every weekend and got to shoot VO's for the Saturday and Sunday newscasts. We used Bolex 16mm cameras that you'd have to wind up and could roll for thirty seconds, and learned about using light meters and some of the technical do's and don'ts. But, really, you just learned from your mistakes, getting your hands in the chemicals, splicing and cutting the film and doing it. It was really good experience and the fact that they paid minimum wage helped pay for gasoline.

I got my first job at KTEN-TV in Ada, Oklahoma, in January, 1976. I knew starting out that I needed to shoot my own stories, so I embraced it. The good thing about starting in a small market is you get broader experience. I anchored the morning news, then reported for later newscasts. Some times I'd shoot for another reporter on their story and then they'd shoot for my story. At other times we were one-man band reporters, shooting our own stories.

I'd go throughout southeast Oklahoma chasing storm damage, or whatever the story of the day was, and getting the film back in time for processing and editing. It was a challenge. Going out on stories, I saw things I'd never seen before. I'll never forget a bank robber who realized he was cornered and blew his head off with a shotgun and a Highway patrolman said, "Yeah, come on up here and I'll show you."

A couple years later E.N.G. (electronic news gathering) started catching on and the station bought some low-budget video cameras and recorders and it all changed, and for the better.

By then I had my eye set on moving up to a bigger market. My first boss had moved on to Channel 4 (KTVY then, KFOR now) in Oklahoma City, where Darrell Barton was chief photographer at the time, and had worked with Hatteberg at KAKE a few years earlier. They were and are life-long friends. In later years he became freelance and, with CBS anchorman Dan Rather, helped to create *48 Hours*. He's since retired. I'd go up on weekends and watch them put together special projects they did on the side.

I'd applied to KAKE-TV in Wichita and I told Barton I was going to be interviewing with Hatteberg. He told me, "The thing about Hatteberg is you learn by osmosis." He meant that you learn by just being around him.

It may sound crazy, but when I interviewed at KAKE the first time they actually sent me out the door with a camera on a story that I had to shoot in their

KTEN reporter Chris Frank (left) in 1976 with Charles Stacey, KTEN's news director (right). with a 16mm Auricon film camera. "I don't miss those cameras at all."

style. Really put me under the gun, making me put a story on the air—and I wasn't even employed by them. It was like, "Man, they have a different way of doing things."

For whatever reason I missed out on getting that job, but I kept in contact with Hatteberg and kept plying my trade in Ada. Later on another KAKE opening came up and I mentioned to Larry Hatteberg about shooting a local house fire at three p.m. and getting it on the five o'clock newscast. He liked that. It showed a quick turn around for the time. This time he offered me a job over the phone.

M y first day at KAKE was October 27th, 1978, and I haven't stopped since. We shot both film and tape at the time. We were assigned CP-16 16mm cameras. Loved those cameras for their size. The station also had three RCA TK-76 ENG cameras—shoulder killers. Heavy steel cameras not built for comfort. Besides the camera we also had to lug a heavy Sony ¾" tape recording deck. Bulky, to say the least.

At the time, most KAKE reporters shot their own stories and were called "one-man bands." You were assigned equipment and a car and were on-call for after-hour spot news. I just remember that I got a company car and a camera that cost as much as my first house.

KAKE reporter-
photographer
Chris Frank
covering a story
with the RCA TK-
76 video camera
and shouldering
the Sony BVU-50
recording deck.

I went through a period where every day I'd take Hatteberg's N.P.P.A. entry tapes into an editing room and watch them while I was having lunch. What I learned from both Hatteberg and Barton were things like sequences and shooting in the way you'd remember how old movies were shot. Hatteberg stressed "rules" to new photographers like not zooming too much. To think in terms of wide, medium and close-up shots. But when I watched Hatteberg's tapes I'd see how he broke his own rules. I'd discuss it with him and he'd say, "When you know the rules, then you know when you can bend them and not abuse them." The rules weren't meant to be The Ten Commandments and you wouldn't suffer the wrath of God if you broke them. It meant having motivation whenever you zoomed or panned.

Up to this time KAKE didn't hire photojournalists who didn't want to report also. Part of that was because of the bulkiness of the E.N.G. cameras at the time. It wasn't long before the station changed and started hiring strictly photographers. I still remember being asked if I wanted to just report or just shoot? I thought if I gave up my equipment I'd also have to give up my company car. I said I'd like to continue the arrangement I had and he said okay.

Then Hatteberg became news director and had to give up his equipment and, as a result, I was the only daily reporting one-man band left.

I've taken my one-man band reporting overseas. I spent nine days in Haiti when we were trying to get Jean-Bertrand Aristide out of the country. I did a two and a half week tour of the U.S. Navy Sixth Fleet in the Mediterranean where I hopped from ship to ship on helicopters, landed on the U.S.S. Teddy

Roosevelt nuclear-powered aircraft carrier, and took off from it on one of their planes. As well, I did other one-man band trips overseas to military bases in Germany and Spain through McConnell Air Force Base here in Wichita.

One time we were in a news meeting and the news director said, "I want to go around and I want you people to think of something complimentary to say about someone else in this room." When it came to our chief meteorologist's turn he said, "You know, I've work here I don't know how many months and in all that time I never knew that Chris Frank shot his own stories, because I watch his stories and they don't look like someone who does them all by himself." And I get that all the time. Maybe I'll go to interview the Chief Executive Officer of Cessna Aircraft or Beechcraft, and the first time I go into their office they'll say, "You do this by yourself?" I wish I got a dollar for each time I get that.

Sometimes people think it's because of cutbacks, but the truth is that I was a one-man band even when we were spending money. I'm not a one-man band out of budget reasons, though I think it gives me some job security that perhaps I wouldn't have otherwise.

There are advantages to being a one-man band, but there are also downsides. When the reporters working in the cubicles around me finish their five o'clock scripts, the photographers they're working with take the scripts into the editing rooms to edit and the reporters go on to writing their six o'clock scripts. Well, when I finish my script, *I* go to the editing room or I work at the laptop at my desk and *I* edit it, and only *then* do I start writing the next script.

I've had news directors who've treated me, as a one-man band, as if I were a two-person crew and would have me scrambling to do a package in one of the early newscasts without any thought whatsoever that I was working by myself. If I made it, I made it. f I didn't, they'd say, "What's the matter with you?" That was the biggest stress to being a one-man band—having supervisors who just did not understand.

Particularly when breaking news happens close to a newscast where it really is important to have two people—a reporter on the phone trying to get information and working with the producers back at the station, while the photographer's shooting whatever's going on for their live shots. At times like those four hands can certainly be much faster than two.

You've hit the nail on the head. Like when I'm doing a live shot and I'm physically editing my video in the live truck. It's so darned frustrating because both hands have to be on the editing machine and I can't even call my supers in. You want your supers in your story, but there may not be time, I might just be pushing it right up to barely getting the tape fed in over the microwave. Then I've got to get my microphone and my IFB on, get in front of the camera, and there's literally no time to tell the producer, "Hey, my locator super is such and such and comes in from zero to five seconds and the next super is such and such." That's frustrating because that's information I want to get to the viewer. I want them to know who the people in the story are. Whereas with a two-person crew, the photographer is editing while the reporter's calling those things in.

Sometimes on a live shot I'm left to say to the producers just before they come to me, "Folks, this is strictly ad lib and we're just going to have to wing it and I'll just say, 'Let's go to the tape.'"

I still do live shots, just not as many as a two-person crew because my news director Dave Grant understands that there are limitations to what one person can do versus what a two-person crew on a live shot can do better. Dave has told me, "Chris, you don't need to be a hero. Don't try to do a package out there if a VO-SOT would work out better." When your boss tells you things like that, it makes being a one-man band a lot better.

Are you given more time to spend on a story since you're putting everything together yourself?

Fortunately, I do usually have that. But there are those days where the calls you've made aren't getting returned and stories that might have come together in the morning or early afternoon fall through and I need to be pressed into doing that late-breaking thing. The key there is managing your time. In those occasions I have to go back to the "K.I.S.S." acronym: "Keep It Simple, Stupid." I'll ask myself, "What do they need to know?" Then I can make that deadline so much easier.

I'll try to keep a positive mental attitude and say to myself, "Let's just take this as a challenge that we're going to meet," rather than let myself think, "Why are they requiring me to make this ungodly deadline when they know that I'm up against the wall?" As long as I can stay positive, then it's almost like being a runner who's trying to shave a second off their track time.

I've developed the realization that my strong suit is trying to do a daily story as well as you can do it that day, let go, then start the next day fresh.

We do these look-live packages a lot where I do a stand-up open and a stand-up close. Even though I'm a one-man band I figured out that I can make my stories look like a two-person photographer and reporter crew story by being creative with my stand-ups. I'll have the camera on the tripod and turn the flip-out monitor on the side of the camera around so that I can get an idea of whether I'm cropped properly, then I'll arrange an opening stand-up so that I'm walking up to the camera as a way to give some movement. And I may do it briskly so that on my last line I'm right there with my eyes two-thirds up the screen where you're supposed to be framed. Now there are people who will recognize me on the street and say, "Oh, you're the guy that charges the camera!" That's become a signature for me.

Do you ever work strictly as a reporter with a photographer?

Usually that's if it's a live shot, where there's another photographer available, but not very often anymore.

My beat responsibility is covering the aircraft industry. Beechcraft and Cessna are based here in Wichita, and Boeing has a big construction facility here. [Air Force One was constructed in Wichita.] Every year there's the annual convention of the N.B.A.A., the National Business Aviation Association, where all the aviation companies come together and show their wares in cities like Orlando, Atlanta, Dallas or Las Vegas. The first time I was going to that we had a wise general manager who told the news director, "Chris is not going by himself. That's too big of a convention for one person to handle." So I always had a photographer because we had to carry so much equipment around on those huge convention floors where there were lots of airplanes and lots and lots of walking. Every year photographers would covet getting to go with me because it was an out-of-town trip.

Well, the past two or three years I've gone by myself. Why? The equipment's changed. I take a laptop to edit with, and FTP the stories back and the station is able to get the look-live stories showing their reporter in another city, which they like. Plus, my camera has gotten so much smaller because now we're digital. That's part of the evolution of news. It's easier to manage now with the lighter equipment and having a laptop.

What kind of camera are you shooting with?

It's a Sony prosumer-size camera. The one drawback is the lens isn't as long. We shoot on SD cards and load those straight into the laptop and edit on Avid Newscutter, but the past two years I've edited on Edius. And we're editing on the server now so we're strictly tapeless.

For the last two years I was editing right at my cubicle and was wired into the system, I was the only reporter in the newsroom doing that. My boss Dave Grant loved that and thought it was the wave of the future.

Photos of KAKE's Chris Frank at work in the field courtesy of Michael Tittinger. (mikeywalks.com)

Since you've been working as a one-man reporter-photographer for thirty years, do you find it simpler because you don't have to communicate with anybody else about how you want to tell the story?

There were many years where I would work with either other reporters or other photographers and the news director or Hatteberg would be stressing to us, "Folks, you've got to learn how to communicate with each other." There would be times where there would be almost knock-down drag-out arguments between reporters and photographers, especially when you get two highly motivated people together who have honest disagreements about the direction of a story. The challenge with the two-person crew is to get their egos working together for the single cause of telling a good, well-rounded story so that the audience—their clients, their customers—are better informed, thereby satisfying both of them and being creative at the same time. It takes creativity to be able to meld those egos together and come up with one voice. I remember times where the photojournalist had a better handle of the story than I did as the reporter and I would think to myself, "I'm going to roll with this. I'm taking their idea and I'm going with it."

Your commitment is still there.

You've got to have that. I don't care what job you're doing, you can't just phone it in. I'm always having these internal discussions where I say to myself, "Come on, Chris, you're a veteran at this. You know the story. Think it through." Then when I get into the editing room and I'm cussing the photographer, it's me that I'm cussing at. "Chris, what were you thinking? Why didn't you hold that shot longer! Why didn't you get such and such a cutaway?" People will be walking by in the hallway and

hear this and be laughing because they know the photographer that didn't get the shot was me.

I want my story to pass muster just as if it were to be picked up by the network. I'm still going to the job that I'm hired to do, because there are a lot of people without jobs and I'm thankful to have a job.

Being a one-man band means you're saving the station money because you're one person doing the job of two people. You must see a certain job security in that?

I do and have actually taken some solace from that.

The key to having happy one-man video journalists is in having educated assignment editors, managing editors, news directors and producers who understand the shortcomings and the time requirements, so that they know when they're asking too much.

But then the other day Beechcraft could only give me an interview at 3:30 in the afternoon and they're on the complete opposite end of the city. I was comfortable enough with the subject that I came back and did the "Keep It Simple, Stupid" thing, just picked bites as I was writing the story. It was the second story in the newscast and I hit my slot with no problem. But my boss Dave Grant noticed this because he knew how late in the afternoon I'd left to get the interview. Afterward he said to me, "Man, how did you turn that story around so quickly?"

That's experience. That's one thing about being a veteran. I've learned some things where maybe twenty years ago I wouldn't have been able to pull it off.

I used to have to work weekends and nightside or come in very early in the morning. Now, for the most part, I have an eight or maybe a nine hour workday, whereas it used to be almost mandatory overtime all the time. I haven't been on overnight callouts in years. And working Monday through Friday, there're things to like about that. I drive home to my house every night. Often I can have lunch at home and still get back to work on time. Having four weeks of vacation off a year, there're things to like about that.

What I'm getting at is that there are benefits to toughing it out. I'm in a better spot now than I was twenty years ago.

WAYNE FREEDMAN: MMJ, KGO-TV, San Francisco, California

Some people call themselves "storytellers" because that's part of what their job entails. For Wayne Freedman, storytelling is in his blood. "When I was a kid in school they gave you ten words and said, 'Make a story.' I could do it in two sentences, if not one." Wayne has been telling stories ever since, for newspapers from the time he was in junior high school, then moving into television once he started college. He's now in his fourth decade in TV, with a staggering 51 Emmys to his credit. He's also generous with his knowledge and what he's learned over the years. He frequently lectures and participates in workshops, cultivating tomorrow's journalists, and he's put what he knows into print in *It Takes More Than Good Looks to Succeed at Television News Reporting, 2nd Edition,* one of the best books on TV news reporting and writing for both journalism students, as well as industry professionals.

How did you get into news?

I grew up in L.A. and was reporting at fourteen years old. They had a high school journalism class in my junior high school—I couldn't imagine not being on the newspaper. They divided up all the beats and the last beat they gave out was to write the daily column for the Valley News and Green Sheet, which is now the *Los Angeles Daily News*. I got that beat and wrote weekly columns about junior high school and high school until I was eighteen years old.

My first job was as a page at KABC-TV in Los Angeles in 1974 or '75, dealing with the audience and the girls and crazies on *Let's Make A Deal*. My dad was a shooter at ABC, the first live handheld electronic camera operator. His first camera weighed a hundred pounds—and that was just the camera, didn't even have a viewfinder. He was famous—Mike Freedman.

He said to me, "If you want to work in television, go work in the news. They will never cancel the news."

He knew some people and after a year of taking care of the audiences of *Let's Make A Deal* I was assigned to the newsroom cutting teleprompter copy for Jerry Dunphy. They had just invented the teleprompter. I cut his scripts together literally piece by piece with a razor blade and scotch tape, spliced them like film, put them through a rolling machine and they'd put it in front of the anchor. I remember Jerry Dunphy saying, "Put a line through every page so I can look down so it looks like I'm reading my copy."

Where did you first get into broadcasting?

In Missouri on the campus TV station, KOMU, an NBC affiliate. By the time I left I was being paid as a special teaching assistant.

The first paying, don't-do-nothing-else, don't-go-to-school, you-are-a-broadcast-professional job was WLKY in Louisville, Kentucky. They hired me as a reporter-photographer, but after six months I realized I wasn't going to be a very good photographer. I hated chasing after all the gear. I got there in January, left ten months later in December and went to WAVE-TV as a full-time, full-on reporter and put the camera behind me. Then I was at KDFW-TV, the CBS station in Dallas for ten months. Then it was KRON-TV in San Francisco for eight and a half years. Then CBS News New York, based out of Los Angeles, for three years as the national features correspondent for *CBS This Morning*. That was a great job, but it cost a lot and they ran out of money. It was the last of the good days of the networks. They'd give out $25,000 a year raises. Finally, I've been with KGO for the last twenty years.

You recently won your 50th Emmy for a story that you shot yourself as an MMJ.

You mean, how does a guy who'd been a photographer for seven months when he was 26 years old come back and win an Emmy?

Yes. This is really going full-circle, isn't it?

Completely full-circle. It was my 50th and, as far as I'm concerned, it was my last. I'd always said in jest that if I ever made fifty Emmys I'd leave. Fifty was just a ridiculous number. I was happy at forty, but people said, "You need to make fifty." And fifty was beautiful. My daughter, who'd been coming with me to the Emmys every year since she was a little girl, was now up on stage as Miss Emmy. The competition was incredibly tough. And I won the damn thing. I couldn't believe it. So I got up there and my daughter gave me the thing with a tear in her eye. I got a standing ovation from the audience. I basically said that I'm done competing, it's time for somebody else. Then I sat down and twenty minutes later I won fifty-one for writing. So now I'm done. Believe me, I'm done.

Taking up the camera again, how has that been?

First of all, I don't get to do it exclusively. I get to do it maybe once a week. For the most part I'm still a news guy and at least three days a week I've got a regular crew, do a regular daily news story. If there's a big, breaking story I'm the guy they send. I'm one of the fastest writers in the shop. They know I can turn it around, get it on, no matter what.

If you're doing one-man band daily news, it's a bear. You can only do one daily news story well that way—and it's probably not going to be the most elaborate story in the world.

There have been a couple of times where they've asked me to do it and I've gone ahead and done it. Were those stories as good? No. There's just too much other stuff that goes into it.

Driving around in a car here in San Francisco, and then adding to that the level of stuff I need to be thinking about. I spend more of my time in the car than I do shooting a story. I've got to think, "Where am I going to worry about parking?" Haul the gear.

Just shooting a stand-up—you don't stand there in front of the photographer and say, "Let's do this." I've got to figure out where I'm going to stand. I've got to figure out the angle, the focal length. I've got to focus on a stick or something on the ground, then walk around in front, use the remote control, turn it on, turn it off. You're looking like an idiot talking into the camera.

I can't have somebody else driving while I'm logging. You can't be taking notes when you're rolling a camera. It's just going to make for a longer day.

Is it as good as anything that's ever been done before with the best photographers I've ever worked with? Not even close.

How about being able to do longer HFR² stories?

For a guy like me who enjoys long-form storytelling, it's opened up vistas that had long gone—the ability to do the stories that I hadn't been able to do for four or five years. They basically said to me, "Look, we know you're not doing the kind of stories you want to do any more because we don't have the staff. If you want to do those stories we'll give you a camera and let you start shooting your own."

I'm not the biggest advocate of daily news one-man banding. I *am* an advocate of going out and telling your story on your own, using the equipment to do it and having control over it—and making a better, more thoughtful piece.

You started training as an MMJ in the spring of 2010 and you won an Emmy in that category the same year?

Yeah, but you have to understand, this is a whole 'nother layer for reporters to have to think about in the field. It's a whole 'nother set of tasks to put in their minds. I assume it's the same thing for photographers who're being asked to report. They know how to do a certain job and now it's like playing chess in two or three dimensions. For the younger generation coming up, they're as comfortable with a camera in their hand as we were with a notepad and pencil.

What made me different is that I used to be a shooter. My father was a shooter. I would see a story in the field and say, "Give me a wide shot here. Give me a compression shot there. I hear a neon light buzzing over here—let's get some sound from that." But, I worked with *great* photographers. Ken Schwartz at KRON taught me pretty much everything I know about long-form storytelling. I worked with really exceptional, artistic photographers. You do that for thirty years and you learn a little.

Also for thirty years, even though I'd put the camera down, I was locked in an editing room and I saw pictures more than I saw facts and figures or subject—I saw storyline. So I came to this job with that mindset. The University of Missouri taught me to be a photographer. They taught me sequencing. A lot of these guys don't even know what a white balance is.

What's your MMJ gear situation?

The camera is a Panasonic something with a card. Weighs about three or four pounds. Tiny little thing. I've put a big, long ME-80 Sennheiser shotgun on the camera. I really want that good sound that allows me to do a quick interview

---

² Hold For Release—A story that does not air on the same day that it is shot, but that will run at a later date, the next day, the next week, or even the month if it's a sweeps piece being used during one of the ratings periods.

with somebody just five feet away and not have to mic them up. And for a quick sound bite it's more than enough. I've got a Sennheiser wireless microphone, and they gave me two lights and a tripod. And I've been grabbing as much gear as I can from my fellow photographers. I've added a big, twenty year-old metal softbox, and my dad left me a couple of umbrellas. He said, "You never know, son, you might need 'em some day." I'd stuffed them in the garage. They'd been there for twenty years. Turns out I'm using the damn stuff.

How much time do you have to work on an HFR story?

It's usually drive to, shoot it, and get back—a one day shoot. The most elaborate shoot was a story I did at a drive-in movie, which was a day and a half. The other half-day was combined with another story with a scientific researcher in Mono Lake. But that was just distance. I finished shooting them in an hour, hour and a half.

How do you shoot technically?

I shoot a lot of sequences. A lot of the classic wide, medium, tight. I remember, always shoot the wide shot. Sometimes you're going to forget it.

If it's a fast-action thing, I'll put it on autofocus and just run with it. The camera itself is so ungainly. I'd rather have it on my shoulder. I like holding it up to my eye and looking through the viewfinder. I don't like using that screen that flips out, because you can't count on it. Your arms get pretty damn tired that way. I use a tripod a lot more than my hands. But generally whatever the situation needs.

Because all the viewfinders are on the left side of the camera, it's a struggle to do interviews with people and not have them facing camera left—because I want some to look left, some to look right, change up the focal length. But all the MOS's are pretty much always looking camera left. This is why nine times out of ten my stand-up will have me walking in from the left side—so I can see it in the flip out screen.

Do you edit?

Yes, I edit all my HFR stories.

I didn't start out with the little stuff. I started out with all the stories I really wanted to do badly and they were all three or four minutes long. My very first story took thirteen hours to edit. I'm a stickler on blending sound and the aesthetics that make a story good.

The interesting thing I find as a one-man band is that, as the reporter, I still find myself cursing the photographer quite a lot. The photographer in me gets really pissed at the reporter. And then the editor gets frustrated with both of them. I'm now bi-polar or tri-polar.

Do you think that maybe ten years from now MMJs will be the standard?

How many two-man radio crews do you see around anymore? I can't see the future, but probably so, with some technology that we haven't even imagined yet. I think the business is going to be faster and lighter, but I don't necessarily think it's going to be terrific.

What is the reporter in you thinking about in the field?

He's thinking about what he's always thinking about—I'm always looking for the story. And I'm still doing exactly that—I just don't have to tell anybody anymore. "There's a moment happening over here—shoot this." I have tons and tons of respect and affection for photographers. But sometimes they didn't understand why I would want them to shoot something and there's no time to explain that this is a small moment, but it could be something that I could build the entire story around. Now, there's been a lot of times when they would have shot something that I would have missed. But I'm still a reporter. I'm a writer. This is just a tool.

My big things are beginnings, middles, endings, main characters, and what I call "Simple Truths and Universal Appeal." If you can put those items in a story and structure them properly, you're going to get viewers every time.

Is doing the MMJ work giving you any more reporter longevity?

To a degree, it has revived my joy in the business. I'm not limited any more. If there's something I want to do, I can do it. I've always been a long-form storyteller. That had stopped. I can see myself doing this another five years, six years, even ten years. But if I retired tomorrow I'd go out and buy my own gear and find something to do in the business because it's fun. It's a wonderful outlet.

I mean, I'm still physically exhausted at the end of the day. It's just more work. Even if the camera's only five pounds, the tripod's another five or six pounds, plus the lights, the setting it up, the moving it around—you're still doing two jobs. If you asked me if I would rather have a photographer out there with me who was really good on these stories, the answer would be yes. But that's not going to happen. So if they won't do it for you, you need to learn to do it yourself. That's the key: if they won't do it for you, learn to do it yourself.

JOBIN PANICKER: MMJ, KSEE-TV, Fresno, California

Jobin Panicker came recommended to me by Wayne Freedman, who frequently speaks at journalism seminars and workshops and is always looking for new storytellers. Jobin has been at KSEE-TV in Fresno, California, where he produces a regular segment called "Jobin's Journal," which he shoots, reports and edits himself.

Jobin is the recipient of two Edward R. Murrow awards and two awards from the Society of Professional Journalists (SPJ) for reporting.

What got you interested in news?

I was raised in Orange County, California, and my family used to watch KCAL-9 News every night where there was a legendary broadcaster named Jerry Dunfey who inspired me. There was something about his ability to connect with people. You'd hang on every word he said and I always wondered about how he did that. Then in high school I did speech and debate and I got comfortable talking in front of people and thought, "Hey, I might have a talent for this. If I could talk to ten, twenty, thirty people, even a hundred people—I could probably talk to a camera."

So I went to Gonzaga University in Spokane, Washington, and got my bachelor's degree in broadcasting. I learned some of the tricks of the trade of how to tell a good story. But it wasn't until I got to Syracuse, New York, to get my masters that I learned how to really write. I did an internship with the local CBS affiliate where they had the traditional reporter and photographer crews, but didn't have MMJs.

I didn't get introduced to MMJs until some of my professors started to say, "Hey, you need to know how to shoot. This might be a situation you're going to run into. So pick up a camera and shoot your own story, bring it in, and we'll dissect it in class."

I get to my first job and that's what they're looking for—WBOC-TV, the CBS affiliate in Salisbury, Maryland, a small town in Maryland on the peninsula. Was there for about a year and a half. I think they called it a VJ there.

This was the first time where my employers handed me a camera and said, "Go out, shoot something, bring some sound bites back and put together a story." I'm like, "Uh... okay." It's a news factory in those small markets. I'd put together a package, maybe two packages a day on two different stories.

You want to do well, but you just know there are going to be so many mistakes along the way because there's so much to think about. Audio that wasn't mixed right. You hope to just at least get through it on your first gig.

We were using Canon XL-1's and XL-2's. They weren't HD but they worked for us. They were lightweight. But when you're doing a story and you're dressed up in slacks and a shirt and tie, you're sweating—you really are sweating. I came at this as a reporter and then sort of picked up photography after it. As far as pressure goes, it was very difficult.

Two or three times a week I'd be on my own, the rest of the time I'd have a photographer. I also noticed that the female reporters were more likely to get a photographer than I was, so I had to learn to "do it yourself."

I watched some of your stories on Vimeo and I was really impressed. You have compositions in your shots that I've always tried to get in my stories— and that I'm still trying to get. How did you develop your eye?

If you think there's composition in my shots it's fool's luck, that's really what it is. I just try to shoot the hell out of a story and hope it all fits. I think I just get lucky.

Was your MMJ work a factor when getting your second job?

The MMJ work was definitely a factor. I was the senior reporter after a year and a half in Salisbury, which tells you something about the turnover in an entry-level market.

I just sent out tapes to all the stations in Fresno and Bakersfield. I thought I had a logical shot at those markets. I was also getting married at the time. My wife, who is an attorney now, and I wanted to find a place where we could settle and test our skills and our abilities. I got lucky that KSEE called me back. I've been here three years and just signed another two-year contract.

How did Jobin's Journal develop?

There've been times where a producer's said, "I want a package here and I want a package here and I want a package here." And I'll say, "I can't give you three versions of the same package. It's not feasible."

Then we had some new management at our station about a year and a half ago and they saw that I had a penchant for wanting to do stories with a little more depth than the stories that we have to put out on a daily basis where we don't have the time. They came to me and said, "We see that you have a passion for this. We think you do a good job at them. So let's give you your own segment." So that's where Jobin's Journal came from.

It's kind of a straight, positive twist on every story. The guy who goes out and spends his own money to help out kids in need. Those kinds of uplifting stories about really good people and the good stuff that's happening out there. I feel that you have a duty to the people you're telling a story about. You want to make sure the pictures are right, the audio's okay, that you tell a good story. Hopefully, it all ends well.

What kind of gear are you shooting with?

We use the DVC Pro Panasonics. They're HD capable and they're smaller. That helps us when doing stories and having to get in some tight corners.

In addition to shooting is editing—and editing can be a mystery.

Editing is a totally different beast. Editing was always a problem for me. And I think I knew why editing was a problem—because photography was a problem for me. That goes to show you how they really do go hand in hand.

A professor told me, "It means nothing if you tell a good story and you shoot it well, yet you edit it horribly. It's not a complete product and you can't showcase your talent unless it's edited well."

Coming out of college you know these text book styles, such as if your eyes are like a camera's lens, when you walk into a room you first see the room, so start with a wide shot. From there you reach for the door knob, so you need a medium shot of the door. From there you go to a tight of the door knob and then your hand on the door knob.

If all you have are a bunch of wide shots, then good luck. I've always been taught, "Wide, medium tight. Wide, medium tight." It's a mantra I chant all the time. If you shoot that way, if you edit that way, your story will be seamless.

You learn so much about how to shoot by having to edit your own material.

And having to do *all* those things—writing, shooting, editing—*makes* you a better journalist. Of course, it's not easy to be well-rounded in any one of those things. It's a process I'm still going through. I know very little about composition, so photography is a process for me. Editing is still a process for me. I watch the work of other good TV storytellers, somewhat mimicking their styles, and at the same time developing my own style. But if you lose something in the editing you've lost the story, I think.

I've watched other people's work and realized, "Wow, there's something about this story that's getting my attention. There's something about the way this reporter is doing this or there's something about the way the photographer is getting these images that makes me want to listen." Like Wayne Freedman—one of these days I'd like to tell a story the way Wayne Freedman does.

Do you see your future continuing as an MMJ, either as an option or because of the way the business is going?

You know, I am challenged with this all the time. In this industry, MMJs can be seen as a second-rate job, as opposed to being a talent and going out there with a photographer. I'm out to prove that you can be an MMJ and you can do good stories. In the future I'd like to make documentaries, that's always been my passion. Documentaries come with their own challenges—I can tell a story in a minute and a half or two minutes, but can I tell a story and keep people's attention for twenty or thirty minutes? An hour? That's a challenge.

Being an MMJ is tough. You go into a press conference and you're on your own. You have to look over the audio, you have to look over the pictures, and you also still want to be a part of the press conference and ask your questions. You still have to be a reporter.

Do I see myself staying an MMJ forever? If it's necessary, I will. But doing it at the pace I'm doing it now—when I'm forty, fifty, sixty? I don't know. Especially when you come back to the station and the producers want three different versions of the same story.

Are you driven to tweet information and feed updates to the website?

Goodness yes. We're having to work in so many different mediums. Let's be honest, if we want to cater to a different audience you have to go to where they're at—and they're on line. They're on Facebook. They're on Twitter. Putting stuff up on Facebook. We have to let them know where we are—if we're at the scene of a crime, if we're at a crash—and that we'll have this story on the air later tonight.

Sometimes people won't even watch TV, so you'll put the lengthy versions of the story on the web. It can be taxing when you're doing all that *and* you're doing the MMJ thing.

People think it's a glamorous job being on TV. It's not, it really isn't. For me, having to get in early in the morning, pitching your stories, calling your contacts, going out, shooting, writing, editing, then putting on your "pretty face" and going into the studio, fronting it in the newscast, then coming back into the newsroom and posting it to the web. By the end of all that you're exhausted. And there will be times where you think, "You know, this isn't worth it." Especially when you consider what reporters and anchors make in entry-level and small markets. Some days you really wonder if it's worth it.

I would really like to impress upon people that two heads are always better than one. Nothing replaces a reporter and a photographer working together on a story. Two sets of eyes on a story is ideal. Though, that doesn't mean one person can't do it. But the more stuff you have one person do, the more diluted the story will be. There's so much to think about. You're wondering if your audio's okay. If your color's okay. Are you white balanced? Are you getting enough shots? Do you have enough B-roll? Have you done any sequences? And at the same time, have you told a story in all this? You come back in and you're having to log it, write it, and you hope that you pull out a good story.

I am a control freak, which is why this MMJ thing actually works for me. I want to see it through from the beginning to the end. I want to make sure that I'm doing the story justice. I want to make sure that I'm doing the people in the stories justice. So being an MMJ might be a natural thing for me.

JACQUELINE TUALLA: MMJ, KION-TV, Salinas, California

All of the interviews so far have been with working professionals who've climbed up the ladder in their journalism careers or who've moved on to new careers outside of TV. This final interview is different—it's with someone who is only just starting out in their career. At the time of this conversation in November of 2011, Jacqueline Tualla had been earning-a-paycheck as a boots-on-the-ground TV news reporter/MMJ for all of five months.

She'd started as an intern at KCRA in 2008 and kept her internship going for over two years. I have to confess that after a while of seeing her always working at a desk in the newsroom, I'd come to assume that she was part of the staff. I never knew that she had been interning all that time and was still going to school full-time, as well as holding down an outside job to pay the bills.

In the summer of 2011, after graduating from Sacramento State University with a degree in journalism, Jacqueline was packing her bags to move. Not to go back home and start looking for a job like so many other college grads, but to head to Santa Maria, in Santa Barbara county on the California central coast, where she had already landed a job as an on-air reporter at KCOY-TV. As of this writing, in February 2012, she had already moved up to sister station KION-TV in Salinas, California.

I won't be at all surprised to find myself working alongside Jacqueline as a colleague at some point in the future..

You can follow Jacqueline on her journey at tualla.com.

What got you interested in news?

I got interested because of my love for writing and telling people's stories. I grew up in Hayward, California, and after high school I immediately went to Sacramento State University, where I got involved with *The State Hornet* student newspaper on campus. My interest was originally in print journalism. Then, because of the Internet, we started doing these little videos where we would recap the news and I would go on camera. Then I was like, "You know, I kind of like this. I love journalism, but why not look at a different avenue for it?" I had a friend, Gia Vang (now a reporter at WDAF-TV in Kansas City, Missouri, after a stint at KEZI-TV in Eugene, Oregon), who had an internship at KCRA, and I was such a big fan of KCRA already.

What year were you in college when you started your internship?

I was a sophomore. I wanted to do it early because I saw so many of my colleagues graduate with degrees with no luck at getting in the business, whether it was print journalism, online or broadcast. I said to myself, "Once I figure out what I'm going to do, which is going to be soon, I'm going to set out and get it as soon as I can." I'd been told by people in the business how difficult it is to get a job, so I made sure to get the experience that would make me marketable.

What was the process like to get your internship?

I filled out an application and they did a quick interview with me over the phone, then called me back and accepted me. I think that's because I focused a lot on my on-campus journalism experience during my interview.

How was it coming through the doors into a real working newsroom?

It was *so* intimidating because KCRA is a big station with a very big reputation. I came in as someone who didn't know much about the business and suddenly I was working with Emmy Award-winning journalists and shadowing photographers who'd been there for decades. I didn't know what a VO was, what a VO-SOT was, what a package was. I spent a few months just learning the language. But I was really intrigued by how the people in that newsroom gathered the news and how they delivered it and made it relevant to people. Once I got there I knew that was what I really wanted to do.

How did the experience of being an intern go for you?

Some people weren't as welcoming to me because they get so many interns. But once I showed that I really wanted it and I really meant business, then they welcomed me. People will help you if you show that you can help them.

You want the people in the newsroom to look at you as a journalist, not just as a student. You want to blend in. You need to bring story ideas. You need to research. You need to know the news of the day.

Prior to interning anywhere you need to know, "Who is the news director? Who do I need to impress? Who are the people who operate the newsroom and make it all happen?" And a lot of it is networking. There are a lot of talented students out there but they don't know what to do. I started networking with people across the country when I was still in college and I still keep in contact with everyone to this day. It's so important.

I also saw interns who came and said, "Oh my gosh, this is not what I want to do." There were other people who'd put all of their money into studying for this career and then found out as they were about to graduate, "This is a mistake for me." It's really something you want to do early on to see if it really fits you.

Your internship lasted two and a half years. Most internships only last one or two semesters. How did you keep it going?

I kept applying for it and I think I showed that I really wanted it and that I was working at it. Every couple of months I would tell them what I was doing. "These past couple of months I've worked on producing. Now I'm shadowing photographers." Or, "Now I'm working on the web." I think they saw that I was continuing to make progress, so they continued to let me do it.

I would show my stories to Richard Sharp and Damany Lewis (KCRA news reporters) and Anzio Williams (news director) and they would say, "You need to be more active." Interns need to do work, show it to professionals, get feedback, and keep working at it.

If you want to be a reporter you need to do everything the reporters are doing. I would go out with reporters and right after the reporter did their stand-up, I would do my stand-up. I would stay the entire shift. As they were writing their story for the air, I would write my version. At the end of the night I would show the script to the reporter, *then* go and edit it into a full package. You know, reporters do that every day in the business, interns need to emulate that and be doing that work also.

In the beginning the criticism wasn't that great. There were times where I thought, "Maybe I'm not cut out for this." I was in college, working very hard, holding down a job, going to my internship about thirty hours a week for free. There were days where I thought I did really good, but the feedback would be, "Well, you should have done this. You weren't as good there so you need to work on that." At the same time, I really needed that or I wouldn't have been able to create a demo reel that was good enough to get a job. You need to have a tough skin to be in this business, otherwise you're not going to last.

Your website says about your resume reel, "I wrote, edited and tracked every piece." So you learned how to edit?

Oh yeah. I learned how to edit using Avid. I learned how to use E.N.P.S. [the station news writing program], and when I went out to student opportunities through the National Association of Black Journalists (NABJ), I learned how to use iNews. By the time I was nearing the end of my internship I was able to say that I knew how to use those programs and I was able to edit.

How well did your college journalism classes prepare you for working in TV news?

At Sacramento State they didn't offer a broadcast journalism degree. Their main focus was on print journalism and that's what my degree is in. It helped in the sense that I learned about the ethics of journalism, what makes a news story, what elements to get and what questions to ask. But I did not learn *anything* about television until I got into my internship. I learned everything about television at KCRA. Broadcasting is a very different form of journalism and I had to learn that from scratch during my internship. Coming from print journalism, I wanted to tell all the information at the beginning. I was writing for the ear and not for the eyes. TV is very visual and I had to learn how to write for pictures.

How important was having your own website?

I saw some people doing it, but I didn't see everyone doing it and I really wanted to stand out. Anzio Williams told me that's what I needed to be doing, so I said, "Okay. That's the next thing that I'm doing." Within weeks I had a website. And it saved me *a lot* of money because I didn't have to make copies and I didn't have to do mailings when sending my work out for feedback or applying for jobs. All I had to do was send an e-mail with a link to my site so people could click on it and see my demo reel. I think it really worked out in my favor.

From the internship, how did you transition into getting a job?

In December of my senior year I sent e-mails out to news directors in California introducing myself, telling them I was graduating in six months, that I would really appreciate their feedback on my demo reel, that I would like to introduce myself in person and could I meet with them during my winter break. I got responses from six different TV stations, so I went on a road trip, met with news directors, and it went very, very well. The goal was to get my foot in the door and get their feedback on what they thought I should work on. Then I said, "Can I keep in contact with you? After I make these changes to my demo reel, can we chat later as I get closer to graduation?" And almost every single news director said yes.

A couple of months later I sent out e-mails saying, "Hi again. Here's a link to my work." One news director wrote back almost right away. He had a job opening for a multi-media journalist and said, "Can you come in for an interview?" He'd met me when I did my road trip, so when I went in for the second time, this time for the interview, I met with his executive producer and his chief photographer.

Actually, while I was driving down to Santa Barbara for the interview he called me and said, "Hey, we're thinking about having you do a live weather hit from one of the beaches. Would you be okay with that?" I said, "Yeah." And they put me on air and I had to do a live shot as a part of my interview! Then a few weeks later he offered me the job, two months before I graduated. I moved the day after graduation and started the job that following Monday.

When you're looking to start a career you have to be ready to go anywhere and for me to land a job straight out of college in California, I am very grateful.

Were you aware that, in all likelihood, you'd have to be shooting your own stories at your first job as well as reporting?

Yes, I was very aware of that. I'd been looking online and had seen that about 90% of the jobs available were for multi-media journalists. And, actually, I wanted to do that on my first job because most of the news directors I'd talked to were willing to train. I don't think that five years from now they're going to be willing to train people on shooting video.

My news director knew I didn't have any experience shooting so for the first two weeks they trained me. They wanted me to get a feel for the newsroom by shadowing producers and reporters and learning a whole lot about shooting. The third week I started going out and shooting VO-SOTs, then I started doing both VO-SOTs and packages and meeting deadlines. As an intern, I had probably done twenty packages spread out over two and a half years. Now I was doing a package every single day as a reporter—and I'm working on two stories at a time, sometimes more. All while also trying to learn the art of shooting—setting up my gear, getting the video, remembering to level out my tripod, white balance—do all these technical things while still reporting on a story all by myself, rushing back to the station, editing the video, and then delivering it live. I'm not even focusing fully on my story at that point, I'm just trying to meet my deadline. That's a lot for someone who's just out of college.

What type of gear are you working with?

I have a Panasonic P2 camera and editing using Edius, which is very much like Avid. And the newsroom writing system is ENPS.

So five months into the job, what is your work day like?

Wednesday through Friday I come in at 2:30 and work to 11:30 at night, and I usually have to do a live VO-SOT for the five o'clock show. As soon as I'm done with that I work on a new story for nightside. At 5:15, I'll drive to the location, which could be forty minutes away, probably get there by six to begin reporting the story, which can take another thirty or forty minutes. Then I have to make it back to the station by 7:30 to 7:45 to give myself enough time to transcribe the interviews, write, edit and get ready to report live. Oh, and take a lunch break, have to squeeze that in somewhere. So sometimes I'm not writing until eight or eight-thirty for the ten o'clock show.

Then on the weekend I work dayside. We have fewer shows and less people on the weekend, which, I think, is the case at most stations. I do a package and a VO-SOT and sometimes more. Each day there's a possibility that I'll have a photographer, but in most cases I shoot and edit my own video. I've also been trained to run my own live shots if necessary.

Have you picked up any shortcuts along the way?

I've learned that if I'm going to an event to get there early. Sometimes, in the beginning, I would wait to talk to people until after an event and it would take forever and I couldn't get that essential person that I really needed on-camera until it was cutting closer to my deadline. Now I get there early so I can knock the interviews out if the people are available ahead of time, then I'll get my B-roll and go immediately.

I do my interviews really quick now. I'm writing down a lot of things as we're talking before we roll, and then I'm only rolling for those essential sound bites. I'm not rolling when I'm asking them, "How long have you been doing this?" and all that other background information. I'm just getting the important things that I need on-camera and writing all the facts down on paper. That saves me a ton of time.

As an MMJ and also having to write text stories for the web, your print journalism background must come in handy?

Absolutely. My story that runs on air is a totally different version than what I'm posting. With broadcast you're writing to pictures, but if you write that way to the web it won't make any sense to the people who are reading it, so I have to take out some of the more conversational writing and make it more straightforward, like a newspaper article. I also have to apply AP Style when writing web articles.

Jacqueline Tualla in her first newsroom as an MMJ reporter—KCOY-TV in Santa Maria, California.

After all the time that you put into preparing for your career, now that you're a full-time, on-air reporter, how does it feel?

I feel really blessed that I do have a full-time job and that I'm doing what I wanted to do. I put so many hours into my internship. There were times when I couldn't even picture doing what I'm doing now because it felt so far away. And now I'm out there working and I'm thinking, "Wow, I'm really doing this." Right now in my career I'm just really looking forward to showing more improvement, getting more comfortable with it.

A big part of it, too, is developing your credibility and getting to know the people in the community. I've joined a committee and I help out in different communities here. And I'm following up with my sources all the time. I think that's really helping me with generating story ideas because people are calling me now. Yeah, I'm the newbie on the block, but I think that's a way that I can help to set myself apart from other people.

A family even sent flowers to me at the station and mentioned me in the local newspaper, thanking me for a story I did on their deceased family member, which was really nice. I mean, anyone in this business can just report, but I'm trying to make a difference. I'm really trying to tell stories that will impact people by getting to know the community. Not just report what's there, but trying to dig deeper.

MY FIRST JOB: TRIAL BY FIRE

Early days in my new career with a 20 pound Sharp camera, 30 pound Sony BVU-110 deck and highly questionable aluminum tripod. The look of cheerful confidence was my best act.

Hitting The Ground Running: KWCH, Wichita, Kansas, 1983

When KWCH news director Steve Ramsey told me I had the job I had absolutely no idea where Wichita, Kansas, was. I didn't even know how to spell it. I'd driven through Kansas a couple times on trips to Colorado or California, but only stopped long enough to gas up the tank. All I knew was that it was flat and four hundred miles wide from east to west. Now it was going to be "Home."

That first Saturday morning in Wichita I got a map and looked up the station's location, which was on the outskirts of town, literally surrounded by farm fields. My wife and I went apartment hunting for a place reasonably close to the new job and signed a year lease by late afternoon, then headed back to the hotel to watch the 5 o'clock news and see what I was going to be in for.

The look of KWCH's news was different from the news in St. Louis, where the shooting style seemed to be to point the camera at something, then zoom in or zoom out. On the KWCH news there weren't any zooms, the shots were more formal, closer to traditional filmmaking techniques. By the time the newscast was over my adrenalin was rushing.

"I know you want to go there," my wife said as the station's credits were rolling up the screen. "I brought a book with me. Go ahead, I'm okay here."

I got into the car and pulled out the map where I'd marked the address of the station. Wichita was considerably smaller than St. Louis and went from city to suburbs to country very quickly. It was dark as I approached the entrance to the parking lot and I had to stop and wait as a family of deer ambled across the road in front of me.

KWCH "cool guy" Ray Unruh in the mid-1980s. Last I spoke with Ray he was a network freelancer with CBS News in New York making frequent trips to the middle east.

By the side of the building a few four-wheel drive Ford Explorers with decals on the sides that read, "KWCH 12 The Look of a Leader," were parked near a side door, telling me that was the newsroom entrance. I knocked on the door and it was opened by Kevin Nunn, the six foot four inch tall man I'd just seen anchoring the news. Weekend staffs are small, and in smaller markets they're even smaller. In Wichita, the weekend anchor also wrote and produced the news. Kevin gave me a quick tour of the place, which didn't take long, then I settled into an editing room where one of the shooters was cutting a story.

This was Ray Unruh, bar none the coolest guy I've ever met. I'll never forget, Steve Ramsey held a staff meeting, ending by saying, "Anybody got any questions?"

Ray started to rise from his chair. Ramsey looked at him, "Okay, what do you want?"

"You got fifty cents for coffee?"

Ramsey took two quarters out of his pocket and put them in Ray's hand.

It was never said, but generally understood, that if you got Ray's approval, you'd passed. For reasons I'll never know, Ray could see right through me, but he took me into the fold from the start. "Pull up a seat." I sat down at the editing station with him and watched as he edited a story he'd shot that afternoon about dirt bike racers. "I hear you're from St. Louis. They're not big into the N.P.P.A. there. I'm not either, but they're big on it here." It would have been obvious to a blind man that I didn't understand what he was talking about, and Ray wasn't blind. Very patiently, he explained every shot he'd made and why he was cutting it the way he was. "We don't do any pans or zooms here. Everything's static. We let all our action go in and out of frame, and no jump cuts. How do you think these two shots cut together? No, I don't think they work either. Let's try these."

Ray made me feel at home. Then I asked him about the cameras they used.

"We use Sharp cameras here. They're industrial cameras. You're from St. Louis so you're probably used to Ikegami's. These are a little different." Ray put a Sharp up on a desk and pointed out all the buttons and controls, then left to go to the bathroom. The second he was out the door, I scrambled for a sheet of paper and wrote down everything he'd just told me.

As I was driving back to the hotel room I was almost sick. "I've made a terrible mistake," I thought to myself. "This is much, much more difficult than I thought." But there was no going back. I was married and had to provide for us. I'd burned the bridges to my old job and transplanted us 400 miles away to a new city and state. I had to make this work.

Into The Field—My First Day Shooting Tutorial

When I officially came in for my first day of work on Monday morning I was introduced, finally, to Steve Ramsey standing in the doorway of his office, which was little more than a storage closet with a desk.

KWCH chief photographer Jim Anderson. The man who made it all look so easy.

"Mike Carroll, I'm Steve Ramsey. How the hell are you? Get settled in all right?"

"Yes, sir. Thank you for this."

"You're welcome."

Steve was a genuine larger-than-life person—a big man with a welcoming smile, wearing glasses and a pressed white button-down collar shirt and tie. When he gripped your hand you felt him putting his trust in you, which made you want to work hard and not let him down.

"I'm going to hand you over to our chief photographer Jim Anderson. He's going to show you the ropes."

Jim Anderson was in his forties, a pipe smoker, and once the seasons started getting cooler he was never without his cardigan sweater. There was a fatherly quality about Jim. He had a way of looking at you, giving you a smile and a nod and saying, "You're going to do just fine." And afterward, you always felt that you could.

"Welcome to Kansas, Mike. We're glad to have you here," Jim said, shaking my hand. "I've got a story for us to go shoot right now."

He led me out to the news parking lot and as I started to get in the passenger's side of his Explorer I asked, "What about the reporter?"

"I'm the reporter on this one. I do a lot of these."

As we drove north out of town Jim Anderson filled me in on the station and told me about how he was a frequent "one-man band," meaning that he was both the photographer and the reporter on feature and general news stories. He had a bi-weekly segment called "Anderson's Kansas" where he profiled different people or interesting or unusual places around the state.

About an hour later, Jim pulled up to a rural farmhouse filled with solid wooden furniture and lace doilies. Jim was doing a profile piece on a retired grandmother who knitted scarves and gave them away to children at the local elementary school.

The first thing he did was set up a light stand with a photoflood bouncing off the white ceiling, giving a warm, diffused lighting (or "soft light") that allowed him to shoot anywhere in the room without having to move the light. Then he clipped a lavelier microphone to the woman for the interview. This was back in the days when wireless microphones were extremely expensive, running $3,000 or more, so Jim was just using a basic Sony "lav" mic that ran by a thin cable back into his recording deck. (This was before the advent of the one-piece Sony BetaCam.)

Jim set the camera up on a tripod and shot an interview with the woman, which ran about seven minutes. His manner was very warm, relaxed and easygoing. Only six or eight questions to get the woman talking about herself, at what age in her life she'd gotten interested in knitting, what she liked about it and why she enjoyed knitting scarves and giving them away to children. Before you knew it, he had everything he needed. He unclipped the microphone from the woman, took the camera off the tripod and began shooting the B-roll, the detail footage of the woman doing her knitting to put the story together later in editing. All of this Jim shot handheld, the detail close-ups of the woman's hands working the knitting needles, the needle points knotting the yarn, her softly lit face as she did her work—all shot with the camera simply balanced on his shoulder.

Another twenty or so minutes of shooting and Jim looked over at me, nodded and turned off his camera. He was done. He thanked the woman, put his camera down and turned off the light. The rest of her family now came into the room, opened some doors onto a dining room and invited us to join them for a home cooked lunch with fried chicken, mashed potatoes and gravy and corn on the cobb. The chicken had come from their henhouse.

On the drive back to the station I asked Jim about the lunch, "Does that happen to you very often?"

He nodded with a smile, "Pretty much. So what do you think of Kansas? You're not in St. Louis anymore."

"Straight Shooters"—Photo of the KWCH photo staff for a newspaper ad taken just a few months after I'd started. I'm on the far left, alongside Ray Unruh and chief photographer Jim Anderson.

Shoot & Move

Back at the station Jim reviewed his tape with me, and I was astonished to see how rock steady all of his shots were. There was no shakiness or bobbing of the camera at all. It was just absolutely smooth. In all my years in the business I've never seen anyone shoot handheld camera as steady as Jim Anderson.

He methodically went over his shooting style, which he called, **Shoot & Move**. He liked the solid image look that you got from using a tripod on every shot, but working that way took too much time, both for the photographer and the subject, and he was too impatient for that.

He'd start out shooting the interview, framing a full head and shoulders shot—not too wide, not too tight. Then he'd break his camera off the tripod and go to the farthest point in the room and start working his way in from there.

"Shoot and move. Get a shot for about fifteen or twenty seconds, then take a step or two over and move in closer, always changing the angle and the background so that one shot always looks different from the next one. Then when you get around to editing them they'll cut together like butter— one, two, three."

- **Wide Shot**—The room with the woman sitting and knitting.
- **Medium Shot**—The woman knitting on the sofa. For this shot Jim kneeled down so that the camera's lens was at about the same height as the woman's eyes.
- **Medium Close Shot**—On the woman's face looking down at her work. This time Jim was sitting down on the sofa with her, shooting her from the side.

- **Medium Close Shot**—Down angle on the woman's hands knitting. For this shot Jim didn't move, simply panning down to get this angle from his same position.
- **Close-Up**—The woman's hands working the needles. Jim kneeled down again and scrunched down, trying to get the camera lens at a similar eye level as the woman's hands.
- **Same Vantage Point**—Jim used the zoom lens to shoot several tighter shots—of the woman's finger tips and the needle points—to get detail of the work. There was no talking during any of these shots so that the camera's Sennheiser shotgun microphone could pick up the little sounds of the metal needle points tapping together.
- **Low Angle, Shooting Up**—On the woman with her knitting work in the foreground. For this shot Jim kneeled down in front of the woman so that the camera lens was just inches from the needle points and the woman could be seen past them. This type of deep-foreground action is called a **Dynamic Angle**.

When Jim had been shooting the woman, at one point she put her needlework down and reached over to a bag at her side.

"Er, uh—what're you doing now?" Jim asked her.

"I'm changing to a different color of yarn."

"Oh, okay. Could you hold on a minute before you do that? You're going to get it out of that bag there?"

"Yes, that's right."

"Okay, let me just move around here."

Jim put the camera back on his shoulder again, angled the camera on the bag of yarn on the other side of her and started the camera rolling again.

"Okay. Thank you," he said to her.

"Can I pick it up now?"

"Yes, please."

She reached into the bag, rummaged around for a few seconds and picked out another color of yarn and put it in her lap. But Jim just kept his camera angled at the bag instead of panning over with her hands. I didn't understand that.

Later when he was going over his footage with me he paused the tape at that shot and tapped his finger on the TV screen.

"You notice I start with the shot on the bag, then her hands come into the frame, take the yarn, then her hands go out of the frame again and I just hold on the bag. That's a shot that I can drop into the story anywhere I want to. I can go from the interview shot of her talking, then cut to this shot and see her hands come into frame and take out the yarn, then go to the close-up of the woman's face from the side, then go to a nice close-up of her hands doing the knitting, or maybe even the neat wide shot with her knitting needle in the foreground. Or, I could go from the neat wide shot to just this shot of the knitting needle bag as her hands come into the frame. That's called a **Transition Shot**. From a shot like that I can cut to anywhere in the story and to anything I want. It's a nice little editing trick and it makes the story look good to the folks at home, too."

When he finished going over his tape he ejected it and leaned back in his chair. "And that's about all there is to it. Other people could shoot the same story and spend all day doing it and get lots of great stuff, but in the end it's still only going to be a minute and a half story. I always say, don't make a big deal about it. Shoot and move. Get in and get out. Do that, Mike, and you're always going to be okay."

When the day had started out and I showed up to begin an entirely new career and phase in my life, I honestly was wondering, "What in the world have I done?"

However, after spending just a few hours with Jim, watching what he did, how easy he was with people, how simply he could light a room and move around to get the shots he needed in a methodical, unobtrusive, no fuss way—he made it all look easy. Of course, he'd been doing it long enough that it was second nature for him. But he also made me feel that I could do this just as well as he could. And I was eager to get started.

Leaping Into The Fray

It was intimidating. The other shooters were four to five years younger than me and already had one or two years of shooting experience under their belts. They were all welcoming to me, as well as being slightly curious why a guy who'd been working at a station in St. Louis would want to come to work there. When they were talking shop I would listen in, but not participate. To be honest, the vast majority of what they were talking about was way over my head. I just tried not to show it, keeping my mouth shut.

One almost constant topic of conversation was the N.P.P.A.—the National Press Photographers Association. Coveted like gold among the photographers were tapes of N.P.P.A. award-winning news stories. Up to this time I'd only lived in St. Louis and the only TV news I'd ever seen had been either of St. Louis or the national network news. I was looking at these tapes from cities like Denver, Minneapolis, Oklahoma City, San Francisco and Seattle, and seeing the work of local TV news photographers using tripods and carefully composed shots, fast-editing and natural sound to tell stories with so much quality that it could be elevated to an art form.

I suddenly felt like I'd spent my whole life in a bubble. I also started to feel that when I'd stepped through the doors of KWCH, I wasn't simply starting a new job, I'd entered into a profession.

After two days of following in Jim's shadow, I came into work on Wednesday morning and he said, "So, Mike, how do you think you're doing?"

"Good. Excited. I want to go out and shoot a story."

"All right. Let's get you some gear and see how you do."

My first assignment was with the health desk reporter and was a story that wouldn't be running until the following week, so the pressure to have to meet a deadline was off. I could just go out and shoot.

I was given the keys to a car and issued some gear. The last thing I did before heading out was to tape a 3x5 card onto the side of my Sharp video camera with typed instructions:

- Turn camera ON.
- White balance.
- Turn ON shotgun microphone.
- Check audio levels.

The story was at an optician's office about a new type of eye examination where a tiny laser beam was shot in through the patient's retinas to gauge their quality of vision. A simple story that any other shooter could have knocked out in 20 or 30 minutes. It took me nearly two hours.

Eventually the reporter stepped in. "I'm sorry, I have to say something. You're taking way, way, way too long with all this. We can't tie up this doctor and his office any longer. You've got to wrap this up."

This was my first big lesson in shooting news: speed counts.

The drive back to the station was very quiet. Finally, I broke the ice. "I know this isn't supposed to run until some time next week. If you could leave a script for me on Friday, I could edit it over the weekend and have it ready for you on Monday morning."

"I can do that."

Sunday was my day off and is also usually one of the quietest days for a newsroom. I came in around ten in the morning, went into one of the edit bays in the newsroom that had a door and sequestered myself. I didn't want people to see that I didn't know what I was doing.

The reporter had left her script and the tapes on her desk. I'd shot two full tapes and back then ¾" field tapes recorded 20 minutes of footage, so I had 40 minutes of raw footage to work with.

The first hour was painfully slow, trying to figure out what all the buttons on the editing console were for, what they did and how they worked. Not to mention how to set audio levels.

By the second hour I'd managed to edit the first fifteen seconds of the story. But I was getting comfortable with the keyboard, how to set my edit points and where the audio levels should be.

After three hours I had just over a minute edited when one of the most experienced photographers popped his head in. "Hey, are you supposed to be in today? The assignment board shows you're off."

"I just wanted to come in while it's quiet and put this story together."

"You're doing this on overtime?"

"No."

A curious look crossed his face. Working without being on the schedule didn't making sense to him. Then he said, "Play it and let's see."

"Well, it's not done yet."

"That's okay. Let's see."

A bit reluctantly, I rewound the tape to the beginning and hit play. When the tape was finished he said, "You shot this?"

"Yeah," I said a little uncertainly.

"Nice stuff. I'll have to watch it."

Then he left and I went back into the newsroom. A moment later I could hear through the door, "Yeah, Carroll's in there on his day off cutting one of those stupid health desk pieces."

"You're kidding. On his day off?"

"Yeah."

"How's it looking?"

"It looks really good."

After four hours I had the story cut. Any other shooter could have easily cut this 1:45 package in an hour or less—and would have only shot fifteen minutes of tape instead of my forty minutes. But I now knew how to edit.

That turned out to be the best story I did for six months.

After that I made it a point to shoot almost all of my B-roll off the shoulder. It would be years before I would shoot a whole story with a tripod again.

The next day of shooting I came back with orange video. This was back in the days before video cameras had automatic white balancing. In TV news, no matter how bad your shooting is, as long as you bring something back and get it on air, you haven't completely failed. Everybody has their own way of learning. For me, I learn by my mistakes. After that, as soon as I turned the camera on I'd take a new white balance before doing anything else. If I moved into a different lighting situation or went from one room into another, I'd grab a new white balance.

I wasn't going to be a good news photographer overnight, so I decided to get there one step at a time. Every week I was going to take one element of the job and focus on getting better at that.

- **First Week:** Shoot on automatic & just get through it
- **Second Week:** Shoot handheld & make shots steadier
- **Third Week:** Record audio on manual settings
- **Fourth Week:** Concentrate on shooting in sequences—long shot to establish, medium shot on the subjects, close-ups on the action
- **Fifth Week:** Editing speed—get twice as fast
- **Sixth Week:** Improve lighting for interviews
- **Seventh Week:** Shoot everything on tripod

Using this systematic approach, within a couple months I became a much more consistent shooter. I was far from being a "good" photographer, but every week I got better than I was before.

On an average we would be given an hour to cut a package. (This is still pretty much the rule today.) After a few weeks on the job and becoming comfortable with the editing machines, I began forcing myself to cut packages in forty-five minutes, then thirty minutes, and then less. I saw that editing was one of the most important steps in TV news. It's the last stage in the process to get a story on the air. If the story misses its deadline, the first place a producer and manager go to is the editor to find out why a story did not made it on time. There can be many contributing factors to this—the reporter and photographer could have been shooting late into the day, they could have been delayed in traffic, the reporter could have taken too long to write their script. But if you fall into a situation where one or all of those problems come up, if you are able to pull a rabbit out of the hat by being able to speed-cut a story that would normally take an hour in twenty minutes—or less than fifteen minutes—then you're going to be the hero of the day. It may not show off your best work. In fact, it might not look good at all, but as long as you make your slot, you will be the golden child.

Editing machine-to-machine on state of the art Sony ¾" U-Matic decks—two channels of audio and straight-cuts only. In terms of technology and computers at the time, the Commodore 64 computer had only just come out.

I'd been at KWCH for about three months when a great moan rose up from the newsroom. Steve Ramsey had put together an evaluation form for everybody to fill out assessing the quality of their work, attitude, level of commitment, self-motivation, and so on, and assigning number values of one to ten. I filled out my evaluation in a corner away from everybody. I was still so new and trying to figure out what I was doing that I found it difficult to give myself much of a value to the station at all. When I completed the form I gave myself a self-evaluation of four.

"Mike Carroll, come on down," Steve Ramsey called from across the newsroom, waving his big arm for me to follow him into his office. "Come on in here and let's get this over with."

There was an air of finality to Steve's word that was not very comforting.

"Close the door and sit yourself down."

I sat down, slouched over in poor posture, just wanting to get over this and out of the station to shoot some obscure meeting at City Hall and hide.

Steve sat back in his chair with my self-evaluation form in his burly fingers, looking over the low numbers that I had given myself. "Mike, I'm looking over your form and I see that you rate yourself as a four. A four, really?"

I sunk a little deeper into my chair. Perhaps he'd decided to cut off this experiment to make a photographer out of me.

"I talked with the assignment editor about your self-valuation and he agrees with me. We both think you're a nine."

I could hardly bring myself to believe what he just said. "A nine? Really?"

"I think we both agree that you're the weakest photographer we have right now, but you're always in to work on time. You've got a smile on your face and a good attitude. Jim Anderson tells you how to do something and, yeah, you might not get it right away but you keep working at it. And you don't bitch and moan about your assignment like a lot of sons of bitches I have around here. When the assignment desk calls you to go shoot something you get up off your ass and you go out the door and go shoot it. No, Mike, I think you're judging yourself too hard. You're a good worker and always working to be better and I see steady improvement in you. I give you a nine. I wish a few more of the sons of bitches I have around here were more like you. Good job. Keep it up." Then he shook my hand and sent me out the door and called out for his next victim.

As I crossed the newsroom I heard different people at their desks say, "I got a six. What did you get?"

"Lucky you. I got a five."

In 1987 I returned to shoot a story about the Workshop. Two-time N.P.P.A. Photographer of the Year Larry Hatteburg of KAKE-TV reviews tape shot by Julio Duran, photographer at KVEA-TV (now Fox) in Los Angeles.

My Formal Education—The N.P.P.A. News Video Workshop

Every spring the Oklahoma State University in Norman, Oklahoma, just 150 miles south of Wichita, hosts the N.P.P.A. News Video Workshop, a prestigious five-day event where the top TV news cameramen across the country come to teach what they do.

Steve Ramsey had worked in Oklahoma City alongside Darrell Barton, who had twice been named the N.P.P.A. TV News Photographer of the Year. Steve had a great respect for the organization and, out of his newsroom budget, paid for all of the photographers to be N.P.P.A. members. Each year he also selected two photographers to attend the workshop, all expenses paid. It was a coveted reward and the best shooters put in their dibs to be chosen. Needless to say, I didn't bother.

One evening on a day off the phone rang and it was Steve Ramsey. "Mike, all the other shooters turned in their requests to go to the N.P.P.A. Workshop except you. I wanted to know why?"

"Well, because so many of the other shooters are so far ahead of me and I know that a couple of your best shooters are really counting on this. I'm just not worthy of going yet."

"Why do you think you're not worthy?"

"Well, because I haven't earned the right to apply to it yet. Maybe next year, but I just don't think I'm good enough for it yet and the other guys really want it."

"Okay, I understand that."

He thanked me, then hung up. Ten minutes later the phone rang again.

"Mike, this is Steve Ramsey. I've thought about it and I want to send you to the Workshop. I appreciate why you didn't apply for it, but frankly, I think you could really benefit from what the workshop has to offer. I think that sending you there is going to make you a better photographer and give you a better idea about what you're doing and what you're capable of doing. So I'm going to put you down for it."

"Okay," I said, stunned. "Thank you."

"It's going to be an eye-opening experience for you. I know it was when I went and, to be honest with you, I've never thought of news the same way since. You're going to come back a different photographer."

(More on the specifics of the N.P.P.A. methods will be explored later in the section on "Shooting.")

The N.P.P.A. News Video Workshop was like a TV news boot camp. Award-winning photographers and network reporters homed in on Norman, Oklahoma, to show their work and share with a packed audience how they did what they did and why they did it that way.

The emphasis of the workshop was about using photography, sound, lighting and editing to tell better stories. To make us stop thinking of ourselves exclusively as photographers and to start thinking as storytellers.

Those who attended were broken into two different categories, participating photographers and observers. For the first three days participating photographers were given assignments to shoot during the 90 minute lunch break. These were mundane things like, "Change a tire," "Use a pay phone," "Take a driving test," which we were supposed to turn into 30-second silent movies using the techniques taught in the morning. We could shoot no more than three minutes of tape and no sound, so that the stories had to be completely visual.

In the afternoon were more lectures, followed by a dinner break, then our three minutes of raw footage was reviewed by the instructors. The best photographers in the country would be going over our work.

"What am I supposed to be looking at here? Is this supposed to be a close-up? Why do you have that bright window behind them? These shots won't cut. How long have you been working in television? Do you think this is the right career choice for you?"

We'd then edit our footage into :30 VO's to be critiqued by the same instructors starting the next morning at 8 AM. For me, though, it was a boot camp. It was also encouraging. Fortunately for me, Jim Anderson and the other shooters at KWCH were already shooting in the NP.P.A. style and had prepared me for much of this. It was a much different, and more painful experience for some of the other shooters who'd been working in the business for years, yet were much more in the dark than I was.

Never having been to college, I was like a sponge to this, absorbing every thing that was being said. The Workshop was about being disciplined in how we used our cameras and approached our jobs. After a week at the Workshop, I came away *thinking* like a professional.

From that week forward, when I went out on assignment with a reporter I could see how a story should be done with a clear beginning, middle and end. Sometimes on the way back to the station I'd discuss story structure with the reporter and we'd both be on the same page. Then I'd get their script and it would almost never be the same story that we'd talked about. The beginning might still be the same, but the middle would now be the end and the end would be scattered all over the place. There might also be paragraphs filled with information that was not specifically related to the footage that I'd shot, leaving me no option except to "wallpaper" the sections with highly generic and generally dull images.

But what could I do? They were the reporters with years of experience and they'd done the heavy lifting of coming up with the words to tell the story, which, in my opinion, is always the toughest job in a news story. It was also their name tagging out the end of the piece, not mine. I'd look over the script, smile and say, "Yeah. Great!" and go cut it.

In contrast, the other photographer who made the N.P.P.A. pilgrimage with me never hesitated to voice his wisdom on reporters, to the extent of loudly dictating how they should rewrite their scripts to follow his concept of how the stories should be told. He'd even say, "Look, this story's going to win a lot of awards." This wound up becoming a net win for me, though, because he became the photographer who the reporters least wanted to work with, replacing me on the newsroom popularity ladder.

There's an old saying that if you want something done a certain way you should do it yourself. As long as I was collaborating with a reporter I knew I'd never be able to put together a story that was told the way I wanted. The only way for that to happen was if I told the story myself—as both the photographer *and* the reporter.

KWCH-TV, Channel 12 in Wichita, Kansas, was my journalism school. It gave me an education and a profession that has carried me for the past thirty years. And I hope a few more to come. That first year in the business is one that never leaves you. It's trial by fire. But it's in the frantic, deadline-defying moments where you find your mettle and take command of the moment that you can feel yourself becoming a professional.

Five years after first walking through the doors of Channel 12, during my final week at the station before heading onto a new job, I worked on a couple of stories that required file tape from stories that I'd shot during my first weeks on the job. Searching through the archives I found that all had notes on them that read:

- Bad video – DO NOT USE!
- Orange video – DO NOT USE!
- No audio – DO NOT USE!
- Carroll video – USE AT YOUR OWN RISK!!!

I used the video anyway. It was my way of showing how I'd come full circle.

JULIE BECKER: Former Reporter, KWCH-TV, Wichita, Kansas

Julie Becker (now Julie Becker-Owens) was one of the first reporters I worked with, after which she never wanted to work with me again. Over time, her razor-sharp edge softened.

A year later when Julie became the weekend anchor and producer, I started taking stories that I'd been sent out to shoot as simple VO-SOTs and turning them into whole two-minute packages that I would write and track as a reporter. Julie will be the first to admit that it had nothing to do with her liking my work, but the simple fact that my doing this meant two minutes or more of the newscast that she didn't have to write.

Julie got a Masters in Journalism at Creighton University, and started her career as a reporter-photographer at a small station in Cedar Rapids, South Dakota. She had never shot or edited video before and literally had to hit the ground running, learning on-the-job. A year later she found herself at another little station in Wichita, Kansas, which was about to be going through a lot of changes.

What was KWCH like in the early '80s before I got there?

It was called KTVH when I started and it was the fourth-rated station in a three-station market. I mean, we were a laughing stock. Nobody took us seriously. It was so far behind the times and so run down and so awful. The owners weren't putting money into it. Nobody cared about ratings. Drove around in broken down pieces of junk. We'd go out on stories and crews from the other two stations wouldn't even look at us. It was a joke. We were nothing. That's why it was so much fun to be part of the transition.

Some moneymen from Hays, Kansas, bought the station and made the commitment to turn things around. They changed the name to KWCH [for Wichita] and we got a huge influx of money. They started to hire people, buy new equipment, new vehicles.

Then there was a change in management and Steve Ramsey came in as the news director and he was like a ball of fire. The new owners said, "Whatever it takes, we're going to turn this station around and we're going to make this station number one. Starting today." Everything just turned on a dime. From then on it wasn't a fourth station in a three station market—it was a horse race and we were galloping. We were going and going and going. We meant to be number one. And we worked at it. It was about that time that you came into the picture.

I remember the first time I was assigned to work with you. A story about a Vietnamese family reunion. The parents were here and they had four of their kids joining them after years of trying to get through immigration. It was a really interesting story. You and I went to their home—and it wasn't much bigger than my car. There were like twelve people there, cooking and celebrating, and nobody spoke English except for one of the sons, but they were glad we were there. It was night and the room was dark and they needed to be lit. Reporting-wise, I could tell the story easily, but shooting it was difficult. I remember I was trying to tell you how to set up lights, and as I recall, Mike, you didn't even know what a light stand was. You didn't understand how the tension screws on the light stand worked. Let alone how to position a light, like bouncing it off a bright wall so it was soft and wasn't glaring into people's eyes. I was so frustrated. Nobody spoke English, the lighting was bad, the situation was tiny—and you didn't know how to run the camera.

And I didn't have the Sennheiser shotgun mic turned on.

Of course, not. Nothing was right.

I had the lavelier mic on for the interviews, but the natural sound mic was off, which I didn't realize because I didn't have an earpiece for monitoring the audio. All the other shooters were insistent about turning the Sennheiser mics off between shoots to save on battery life—because they cost a whopping $3 each back then. When we got back to the car and were loading up the gear I saw the red "Aus" [German for "Off"] button on the Sennheiser shotgun mic *and only then did I realize that I'd never turned it on. You didn't say a word to me the whole way back.*

Oh, I was mad, mad, mad, mad, mad.

When we got back I mentioned this to Ray Unruh. He said, "Yeah, that's happened to me, too. Now I just never turn it off. The battery's good for six months or a year anyway." From then on I never turned the Sennheiser off—and I still don't.

It's a great lesson. Hard way to learn it.

KWCH reporter Julie Becker with special projects photographer Jeff Hardeman on a special assignment in Los Angeles in 1987.

You also gave me a valuable lesson in E.N.G. equipment maintenance. We arrived at a news conference in a tiny office at Wichita State University and I went to turn on my Sony BVU-50 recording deck—and it wouldn't turn on. No power. Yet I knew it had a good battery in it. Do you remember what you did?

Picked it up and dropped it from a height of four inches on its right hand corner.

I couldn't believe you did that! Then I couldn't believe that it worked! After that I wound up doing that so many times.

I don't remember who taught me, but obviously I learned the hard way, too. But you got better and you learned things. You learned them on the fly really. As I recall, you were a pretty decent, mediocre photographer. You were up to a point where you just got by, then they sent you to school.

Yes, to the N.P.P.A. Workshop in Norman, Oklahoma.

And when you came back it was like night and day. I wish I could have gone to that school because when you came back it was like somebody had flipped a switch. Suddenly, you knew exactly what you were doing and how to do it. I'd go on an assignment with you, you knew how to call the shots and you knew exactly what it would take to put a story together. And you were thinking like a reporter. You knew when we didn't have a shot that we needed and you knew how to get it. You'd say, "I can't put this story together if I don't have a transition shot." Because we were big on clean-looking stories in those days, you couldn't have jump cuts.

Nowadays you can jump all over the place, do anything, but back then, "You need this shot. You need this shot. You need a transition and then you can go on from there."

Then you started doing your own thing as a one-man band, because you are a storyteller. When photographers and reporters go out together sometimes the photographer has one thing on his mind and the reporter has another thing in mind, but it's really important that they think together to make the story really happen. And I never ever felt that with anyone but you, Mike. You were able to see the whole story—not just from a photographer's point of view, but from the reporter's point of view also. So in your mind you were putting the story together, as was I, and that's why I thought you were a really good storyteller.

Well, I was always thinking about the beginning, middle and the end.

Exactly! And you know, to this day when I work with journalism students and speak to classes, I always tell them, "It has to have a beginning, a middle, and an end."

Ramsey used to hammer into us, "We do not end with sound bites. That's the coward's chicken shit cheap ass way out. You, as the reporter, put it together and wrap it up like a package with a beginning, a middle, and the end. And the ending is the hardest part." And it is, it really is. The ending is so very difficult. It doesn't mean you go to the beginning and the middle and go, "Okay, I'm done." No, you find a way to end it and wrap it up.

I can remember more than once going into Ramsey's office and saying, "I'm ending this story on a sound bite." And he'd say, "If you do that I'm firing you."

Jim Anderson at the editing bay of his production company, Videoworks.

Follow-Up: JIM ANDERSON

In 1987, three years after I was sent to the N.P.P.A. Workshop, KWCH chief photographer Jim Anderson left TV news to form his own production company, Videoworks.

In an ironic twist of fate, when he left, I stepped into his shoes as chief photographer. The guy who didn't know how to run a camera became the person who ran KWCH's news photography department.

On Jim's last day at KWCH, I shook his hand in gratitude for everything he'd taught me. Again, he gave me his reassuring smile and said, "Mikey, you're going to be just fine."

In the final stages of writing this book I was privileged to be put back in touch with Jim, who is enjoying retired life in Phoenix, Arizona. To this day, though, he's still active with cameras, doing photography, video and maintaining the website for his church.

I e-mailed him some of the early chapters to get his reaction. This is part of the note he sent back, which touched me deeply: "Mike, I was just telling Polly that you were that 'new kid' when you came to 12. The other guys would ask why we would hire someone with so little experience. I told them that Steve and I had talked about it and we saw something, potential to be excellent. We were correct. As time went by, you became one of the best, if not the best shooter I had. Now look at you—a long career that's advanced to very nice things. Nice going, Mikey!"

SHOOTING

If you don't like what you're shooting—nobody else will.

SHOOTING TIP: Always smile when looking through the viewfinder. (Obviously there are exceptions to this, such as when working on a tragic story or in a sensitive situation.) When people see you smiling it helps to put them at ease. A reporter once said to me, "I love watching you shoot because you always have the biggest smile on your face. You look like you're really happy to be here."

PEOPLE OFTEN FANTASIZE ABOUT LEADING NOMADIC LIVES OF ADVENTURE. Traveling to exotic places, seeing new things and taking pictures of them. To some degree, you get a sense of that wanderlust working in news. It's certainly unlike the job I used to have, doing the same thing inside windowless walls day after day.

I come to work and load my news gear into a live truck or four-wheel drive and head out to a press conference at City Hall, a snow storm in the mountains, or an interview with a Nobel prize-winning scientist. Working in news you get to see more of the world you live in and how it works than almost any other job I can think of.

Shooting Speed

A photographer with a good eye is a plus, but a photographer with a fair eye who can shoot fast can be twice as valuable, maybe four times.

I don't know if there is such a thing as being born with an eye for photography. I've yet to meet a photographer who didn't start out rough and only got better by working at it. Being able to arrive at a scene ready-to-go, start shooting almost immediately, get the shots quickly and efficiently and move on doesn't happen in a day or a week. It happens over time and through repetition until it's being done on automatic. Then one day you're just doing it, like a pro.

Shots And Clips

Tapeless digital video cameras record shots as "clips." When you press the camera record button, it starts the clip. When you press the button again to stop rolling, the clip is created. A clip can be ten frames long or ten minutes. Quite often these are in the form of QuickTime clips, or .mov files. They can be just a few megabytes in size, as with a quick shot of a few seconds, or extremely large files of several Gigabytes, such as with an extended interview. On an average, a news story will be twenty-five to fifty clips in size.

Once the clips are loaded into the computer and into the folder or bin of the editing program you're working on, they appear as lots of individual files.

The Three Basic Elements of Shooting

There are three essential shots in visual storytelling:

- **Long Shot**—A full view of a scene shot from a distance to establish a location.
- **Medium Shot**—A closer view on a specific area.
- **Close-Up**—A person, object or piece of action going on in this space that you want the viewer to focus their attention on.

An example of these shots used in a sequence of a person in an office typing at a computer, which is a situation that I find myself shooting quite a lot, could be:

Long Shot—Establishing an office with people working at computers.

Medium Shot—A closer angle focusing on one person working at their computer.

Close-Up—A tighter view puts emphasis on the person's face as they work at the computer.

Followed by **A Series of Close-Ups** of the person's fingers moving over the keyboard of the computer, and a separate close-up on the computer screen itself.

In & Out Of Frame Action

This is a well-established method of covering action that goes back to how the classic Hollywood studios would film scenes. The old motion picture cameras were extremely heavy and difficult to move and didn't allow the cameramen to look directly through the lens, so they had to film scenes in shots that were "static," meaning they were locked down and didn't move. Instead, the actors moved through the scene, going in and out of the camera's "frame." Many different angles were then edited together in such a way that the audience never noticed. This shooting technique was carried over into newsreels and on into TV news.

Here's an example of putting this to use when profiling a track and field athlete—the type of story that I've shot many times over the years. A quick, one-stop-shopping assignment that can be knocked out in 45 minutes or so.

An opening sequence could begin like this:

Close Shot—Running shoes being tied.

Close Shot—On the runner tying her shoes, then rising up and **out of frame.**

Wide Shot—As the runner steps **into frame** and kneels down at the starting point.

Close Shot—On the surface of the running track as the runner's hands come into frame.

Close Shot—The starting block as the runner's feet step into frame and get into place.

Close-Up—The runner's face coming into frame as she kneels down into position.

Low Angle Shot Behind Runner—The runner starts off down the track.

This will be followed by a series of angles of the athlete taking off from the starting block, but not running very far.

By shooting the runner stepping up to the starting block, getting into position and taking off in every shot I am giving myself lots of editing options. I can use any of these shots for the opening shot of the runner getting in place for the starting gun, or I can start right out with any one of the shots of the runner taking off. Since she is doing the same thing in every shot, **repetitive action**, I have plenty of match-editing points that I can cut on. What shots I don't use to start the story, I can use in any number of variations throughout the package.

Since this story is about a runner, I'll also need some running shots. For these I simply ask the athlete to run around the track one time. I'll set the camera up on a tripod in the field inside the track where, from a single position, I can use the zoom lens to grab a variety of shots:

Medium Long Shot—The track, then the runner runs **into frame** from the side. I **pan** with the runner for ten to twenty seconds before allowing her to run **out of frame.**

While the runner is going around the track, I'll rapidly pan ahead and zoom in on the track to get a **tight telephoto shot** as the athlete's feet run **into the frame**. I'll then pan with the feet, slowly tilting the camera up to a **medium or medium-close shot** on the athlete to see the detail in her face as she runs. I'll hold on this shot for fifteen to twenty seconds, then quickly pan ahead again and zoom out to frame up for a **long shot** as the runner races **into the frame**. I may lock this shot down as a **static shot** to allow the runner to run through the picture and **out of frame**. This could serve as a good final shot for a sequence, from which I could cut to an interview bite or some other location. As the runner does her lap around the track, I will continue grabbing shots in this way, allowing her to run **out of frame** from one shot, then quickly panning ahead and changing the framing of the shot with the zoom lens, from a **long shot** to a **tight telephoto close shot** and vice versa, until she has completed her lap around the track.

For a final shot I may take the camera off the tripod and run over to get a final **handheld shot** moving with the athlete as she cools down and just leave the camera running for 30-seconds or a minute, as a way of closing out the story.

Framing The Interview

On the subject of the interview, I'm going in reverse-order here as we typically shoot the athlete's interview first before the athlete actually starts working out and getting sweaty. I'll set up in a quiet place away from any kind of activity, in order to get clean sound, and position the person with their back to the sun so that they are backlit with soft, even lighting on their face.

I'll set up a basic shot in advance, which I'll then tweak once the person to be interviewed arrives. The initial shot was perfectly usable, but I felt the background was too bright and contrasted with the woman's face, which is where the audience's eyes will be looking, so I made a quick adjustment to the tripod.

Photos of track & field athlete Chelsea Rodgers, Elk Grove, California.

I lowered the camera about ten inches to frame her head and hair against the darker stand of trees in the background, which are also shadowed. The rim of backlight on her hair provided some separation from the darker background, making her stand out better in the shot.

By having the camera about twenty feet back and being zoomed in, the background is nicely out of focus, accentuating the athlete as being the center of attention in the shot. The use of telephoto also transforms the harsh line of a chain-link fence that runs through the background into a pleasing blur.

White Balance In The Shade

White balance is how the camera is color corrected so that the people in the video don't come out looking blue or green, which can happen under different lighting conditions such as shooting in sunlight, then following someone through a doorway into artificial lighting.

There are buttons or menus for white balancing on all video cameras and digital still cameras. Almost all digital cameras offer automatic white balancing, and I must say that these can be amazingly accurate. When I'm starting out with a new camera I tend to go with the auto features until I become more familiar with it.

However, I don't think anything beats a manually-set white balance. With a manual color balance all of the color in the shots will match and there won't be any color shifts, which you might have if you move from shooting in direct sunlight into the shade of a building or a tree.

When you're starting out in the business and learning about white balancing, the first impulse when shooting outdoors is to look for something white in the sun—a white wall, white T-shirt, white socks, a white car—and grab a white balance off it. That's fine as long as everything you're photographing is also in the same direct sunlight. However, once you swing the camera around and shoot into the shade of a tree or a building the shaded areas will have a blush tint because it's a different color temperature.

Personally, I've never liked the color I got from white balancing in direct sunlight. Everything looked somewhat metallic. One day I asked a shooter who I admired how he always got such rich, beautiful color in his shots. I wondered if he used a special filter or gel over his lens. "I know what you mean. I had the same problem myself," he told me. "Then I tried white balancing in the shade, and now that's all I do. No special filters. No gels. I just white balance in the shade."

It sounded too simple. But right then and there I swung the camera around, grabbed a white balance off the shaded side of a white car and finished shooting my assignment. My camera had a black and white viewfinder so it wasn't until I got back to the station, popped my tape into an edit machine so I could see how it looked on a color monitor. And to my total amazement it was exactly the tonality of color that I'd been striving for. By getting the white balance off something white that was in the shade and *not* in the direct sunlight it meant that everything that was in in the shade and the shadows was the correct color, and also gave everything in direct sunlight a slightly warmer, amber quality. I could then shoot in *every* direction and *everything* would be pleasing to the eye.

The N.P.P.A. Way—Keep It Static & Think In Sequences

When I first started in the business, the shooting styles were heavily influenced by the disciplines established by the N.P.P.A.—National Press Photographers Association (nppa.org).

News was photographed using fixed, locked down shots, even when shooting handheld. The only instances where panning the camera was acceptable was if you were following a person walking or a car driving down the road or a plane touching down. The purpose of this was to make you **Think In Sequences**:

- **Wide Establishing Shot**—A house fire with fire trucks in the foreground and the burning or smoldering house seen beyond them.
- **Another Establishing Shot**—The house with firefighters shooting water into the windows and onto the roof.
- **Closer Shot**—The front of the house as streams of water shoot into the smoke and flames pouring out of the house.
- **Medium Shot**—Firefighters holding fire hose, spraying water.
- **Tight Close-Up**—On front of nozzle with water shooting out.
- **Medium Shot**—From behind firefighters to show water arcing out of the fire hose and in through the front windows.
- **Close-Up**—The battalion chief talking into his walkie-talkie directing the attack on the fire.
- **Close-Ups**—Neighbors standing on their front yards watching.
- **Wide Shot**—From behind neighbors watching this scene.

This solid production technique makes footage look clean, professional and organized, almost like watching a movie. I still think and work this way to this day, thirty years after it was drummed into me.

I encourage everyone interested in television journalism, both student and professional, to become members of the N.P.P.A. for at least the first few years. Whether the goal is to remain as the photographer on your stories or to move on to exclusively reporting, TV news is a visual medium and the more you understand about the camera, sound and editing, the stronger your storytelling will be.

Epiphany—Going My Own Way

The N.P.P.A. shooting rules had given my work a visual foundation. But after fifteen years of following that method, I began to feel stale and that my stories were routine and dispassionate.

I felt a hunger to seek out different ways of seeing and telling stories. I found myself drawn to the BBC World Report and how they held on shots longer, allowing the viewers more time to appreciate the pictures being presented.

I needed to let go of the reins of the camera and recast myself in a new mold—one that I needed to create for myself. Call it mid-life cameraman crisis. I needed to think and see in a new way—following my own rules.

"Active Camera": Shooting Sequences All-In-One Shot

I was at Pier 39 in San Francisco shooting a story about tourism and the economy of the Embarcadero. I'd shot a series of static location set-ups on the tripod to create a quick-cutting sequence of tourists on the Pier. Then I swung the camera around and grabbed a shot of a sightseeing boat pulling out from a dock. By complete accident I left the shot rolling on for a full minute before I realized my error and clicked the camera off.

Later in the afternoon the story was moved up from the six o'clock news to the five o'clock, slashing my edit time down from an hour to a mere fifteen minutes to cut the entire 1:40 package.

I frantically cut together the A-roll with the reporter track and interview bites, then started covering with B-roll. I was down to the wire and had a 20-second "black hole" to fill. I had no time to shuttle around looking for five or six shots to create a sequence. I cued up the mistake shot of the sightseeing boat pulling out of the dock and just let that one shot play over the whole 20-second gap. A few minutes later as I watched the finished story being fed back to the station I was struck by how well the long-running shot of the sightseeing boat worked. It was locked down and nicely framed and the movement of the boat held the viewer's eye. This accident wound up being an epiphany for me.

Starting the very next day, after I'd finished shooting my series of static shots for creating sequences, I'd shoot one additional long-running shot of the scene, "just in case." When I was editing I also experimented. Instead of using the shorter sequenced shots I tried only using the longer-running shots. Playing the stories back, I felt the stories were more audience-friendly with shots that gave the viewers time to really see what the reporter was talking about.

Then it occurred to me that since I'm shooting people in motion, then why shouldn't my camera also be in motion? After that, if I was shooting a sequence of shots of a person working at their computer, I'd shoot one additional long-running handheld shot of the same thing, only this time all of these shots—the long shot, the medium shot, and various detail close-ups of the action—would be in one continuous shot. I'd start with the camera in a long shot, then move forward into the medium shot and on into the close-up, panning into other close-ups of fingers tapping at a keyboard or operating a mouse, then pan over to the computer screen. I'd then reverse myself and move backwards into the original establishing shot. The advantage to this was that later in editing, if I was up against a deadline I could cut into that long-running shot from anywhere and let it run to "fill the donut." Furthermore, where it once took me thirty minutes to speed-cut a package, I could now jam one out in just ten or fifteen minutes.

After a few weeks of shooting like that I stopped shooting static sequence shots entirely.

This style was also applied to establishing shots of buildings and locations ("real estate shots"). Before I would shoot these as:

Long Establishing Shot—A building.
Tight Telephoto Shot—Name of the building above the entrance.
Medium-Long Shot—The front entrance of the building with a smooth tilt up of the building, followed by a smooth tilt back down.

Now I shoot "real estate" by beginning with a long shot, then zooming in on the building and the name. A zoom has the psychological effect of making the eye feel that something is happening. A single, slow zooming shot of an empty field can hold the viewer's attention for ten or fifteen seconds or more because the subtle motion of the zoom keeps the viewer's eyes stimulated.

"There Is No B-Roll—There Is Only A-Roll"

I once attended a workshop where Ray Farkas, a producer of news and documentary programming for NBC and PBS, began his presentation by saying, "I hear a lot of people talking about B-roll. For the kind of work I do, there is no B-roll—there is only A-roll"

Farkas specialized in telling complex stories without a scripted reporter track, but entirely through interviews and natural sound. He also had a signature style of putting wireless mics on people, then recording what they said from across a room with a locked down, static camera.

"There is no B-roll." Those first words really struck a chord in me. Too many times I've had to cut footage that was utterly lifeless. Static shots where nothing was happening that played like a slide show. Other times I've worked with footage that seemed like it was shot using a stopwatch— roll for five seconds, stop, change angles, roll for five more seconds, stop, get another angle, and so on. Plenty of shots, but absolutely no interest paid to the people or the action that was happening in the shots. Just, "Get a wide shot here, a medium shot there, some tighter shots. Okay, let's go." In both cases, there were plenty of shots to cover a track with—but absolutely nothing that was worth watching.

After hearing Ray Farkas' words, I understood why those shots weren't worth looking at—because they'd been treated like second class material. Farkas felt that every shot should have value and be regarded as a primary shot.

"There is only A-roll" has stayed with me. Every time I press the record button I'm aware that it will most likely be used on-air as B-roll, but I always shoot it as if it will be seen as A-roll.

Every time I look through the viewfinder and frame up a shot I think, "Can this shot hold up on it's own? If there were no reporter talking over this shot, would it be interesting? Could I cut from an interview or a reporter stand-up to just this shot and let it hold on its own with only natural sound for the two to five seconds that it will play on the air? Does this shot matter?"

GEAR

First Job Cameras

IN YOUR FIRST ENTRY-LEVEL JOB at a small market station, the resources are going to be limited so the equipment will probably either be industrial or prosumer (professional consumer) grade, which can still be very good and put out very high-quality pictures.

Pick the brains of your colleagues about the equipment and test it yourself to find out:

- How it handles in low-light and at night.
- How long the batteries last.
- If there's a battery charger that can run off a car's cigarette lighter to recharge batteries.
- If you have wireless mics and how far they'll transmit.
- How sturdy the tripod is.
- If you can pan smoothly with it or will it only work for fixed, locked-down shots.

You may also have to share gear—one camera for two or more people. If so, make an inventory of everything and where it all goes. When you finish at the end of a shift, make sure it's all there and back in the right place.

SHOOTING TIP: Always carry a quarter with you. It works perfectly for tightening the bolt of a tripod plate. (And might come in handy for parking.)

At my first station I worked with two Sonys and a Panasonic. The most challenging was a very small Sony camera that was difficult to get a steady shot off the tripod. So if I had to move the camera I would lift and move the tripod with the camera on it and that made it steadier. I don't know how other people do it, but that's how it worked for me.

ASHLEIGH WALTERS, WPTV-TV,
West Palm Beach, Florida

KCRA reporter Tom DuHain taking Android photos while on a story for the kcra.com website.

Little Cameras—Secret Tools

A fellow photographer was working on a story about an NBA player who'd been charged with illegal dogfighting. He went to the animal shelter where the player's confiscated dogs were being held and was told, "We'll talk to you, but we don't want any filming in here with any big news cameras."

"No problem," my friend replied.

He was then left alone in the lobby while the director of the shelter was being summoned. He took out a small compact camera, set it to video mode and recorded several shots of the interior. None of the dogs in question were visible, of course, but it was a little extra video to help fill the holes of the story. It hadn't been shot with his "big news camera," so he'd kept his word.

A small pocket camera, or an iPhone or Android, that can shoot high-quality video are valuable tools. Just because they aren't a "big news camera" doesn't make them any less valid.

Some of the most important footage documenting the social upheavals in the Middle East were shot with cell phones and uploaded to Youtube for the world to see. These can sometimes be more effective journalism tools because they're not taken seriously, making them more invisible.

Media Credentials

I always thought the scenes in old movies of hard-boiled reporters with "PRESS" cards stuck in the bands of their fedoras were nothing but Hollywood shtick. It wasn't until I became a "member of the press" that I discovered it was all true.

Media credentials, in most states, are issued by the state highway patrol, the local police, sheriff's department or city hall. Every municipality is different. Most state legislatures and governor's offices issue their own credentials as well.

To get credentialed you fill out an application form stating:

- Your name
- News organization you work for, work address, work phone and manager/supervisor contact info
- Birthday, weight, height, eye color, ethnicity
- Driver's license number
- Social security number

A newsroom manager, the news director or the business office provides a signed letter on company letterhead confirming that you work there.

The credentialing agency takes an I.D. photo of you and you might be fingerprinted. A laminated media credential is either given to you at the time or mailed to your officer. Then you're official.

This is also necessary for freelance and "stringer" journalists.

This comes in extremely handy when arriving late to a governor's or senator's press conference, as well as through some police and fire lines, and all the proper credentials are dangling from your neck.

Tools Of The Trade

Up to just a few years ago TV news cameras cost anywhere from $30,000 to $60,000. During that time I demonstrated how for under $5,000 you could shoot news with a $2,500 camcorder, using the same high-end microphones that I use every day on my $50,000 news camera, load the footage into a MacBook and edit it on Final Cut Pro. The story aired on the evening news and was, so I was told, one of the best looking stories in the newscast. Now this has become the norm for MMJs across the country. These are examples of some of the essential gear that you'll be using or might consider investing in.

External Shotgun Microphone

A general purpose mini-shotgun microphone that is standard issue with most camcorders. I've used one on my Sony XDCAM news camera for years and I'm continually surprised at the quality of sound it produces.

Fuzzy Windjammer Windscreen

As good as mini-shotgun mics are, their biggest weakness is wind, even with a foam windscreen. I highly recommend using a fuzzy windjammer that slips on over the foam windscreen. You'll be amazed at how much cleaner the sound is on a windy day. These can be found on eBay for around $30.

Sennheiser ME66 Shotgun Microphone

This is the industry standard shotgun microphone for news. There are quality name brands other than Sennheiser that are higher and lower in price range, but I regard Sennheiser as the gold standard. You'll be hard-pressed to find another microphone as rugged in all kinds of conditions than the ME66—not to mention delivering excellent sound all the time. And they last forever. It's not uncommon to find a Sennheiser microphone that's twenty or thirty years old and still working perfectly.

Sennheiser ME66 shotgun mic without a foam windscreen cover.

Rycote Softie Shotgun Windshield

As hearty as the Sennheiser ME66 is, its Achilles heel is wind. The Rycote Softie is the best protective wind screen that I've ever used. I'm not a gear junkie, I try to keep my gear to a minimum, but the first time that I saw one of these on another shooter's shotgun mic I had to have one. The very first time I used it was in a high-wind snowstorm in the Sierra Nevada mountains. I was shooting an interview alongside a reporter who was using a wireless stick mic, which is generally reliable in almost any type of condition. I was amazed to hear that the sound coming from the Sennheiser with the Rycote Softie windjammer was absolutely clear. In fact, if it wasn't for the wind blowing snow sideways in the background you'd have thought it was a perfectly calm day.

Sony Stick Microphone

The essential hand-gripped microphone that everyone associates with a reporter doing a live shot or an interview. It has a wire-mesh screen over the audio element, making this microphone highly resilient in hard rain and strong wind situations, and doesn't require a battery or power supply. A workhorse of a mic and virtually impossible to destroy. The base has an XLR jack for plugging into a hardline cable or a wireless transmitter cube.

Sony ECM-55 Lavalier Microphone

Another industry standard. A lavelier mic with a thin cable that plugs into the camera's XLR input jacks. I've carried a Sony ECM-55 lavelier mic in my gear bag for twenty years. Whenever I need a second lav mic or my wireless lav mic is giving me

problems, I pull out the Sony ECM-55 and it never lets me down—provided the AA battery still has a charge.

Wireless Mics

Radio microphones are one of the staples of modern television journalism. For over a dozen years I used a high-quality analog wireless transmitter and receiver and on the best days it would only transmit clearly for about forty feet. Then a few years ago we switched to digital

wireless mics and it was night and day. I could suddenly get a perfect signal from a mic that was a block away or on the other side of walls.

Personally, I own a Sennheiser Evolution G3100 wireless and transmitter, for which I paid $450. A far cry from the $1,500-3,500 price tag in the analog days.

There are few things that can make your stories stand out better than clean audio. If the equipment at your first station isn't up to scratch, dip into your credit card and invest in yourself. You can always resell it on eBay when you get to your next station where, hopefully, the equipment will be better.

Some makers of higher-end news cameras have wireless mic receivers built into the camera's body. This is a Sony lavelier wireless transmitter for the Sony XDCAM camera.

Another essential is a wireless cube transmitter, which serves as the base for the stick microphone.

There is usually a square or triangular "flag" on the stick microphone displaying the station's call-letters—WNBC, KCBS, Action 9 News, etc.

NOTE: These mics get easily scratched over time and use. Periodically we'll pull out a can of black spray paint to touch them up. I use gaffer's tape around the stem for a better grip.

Earphones

Always monitor your audio when shooting.

Occasionally, I'll pull out a big pair of Sennheiser headphones (around $120 or so) with large earphones that cup around the ears. In a loud environment these can cancel out all the other sound around me so that I can only hear what is coming out of the microphones. These headphones isolate the sound so completely that if someone who isn't mic'ed tries to speak to me, I have to lift up one of the headphones in order to hear them. Although, as great as these headphones are, they are also big and can attract attention.

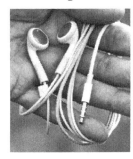

When I'm working on a daily story and just trying to blend in as much as possible, a simple pair of inexpensive iPod-style earbuds work just fine. They're small, innocuous and still allow me to hear the audio of what I'm shooting.

POOR MAN'S LENS SHADE—When the sun is at a steep angle and the sun is flaring into your lens, the strategically placed brim of a baseball cap, or even a reporter's notebook, can be just the trick to keep a blue or green shaft of sun flare from going right across your face during a one-man locked down stand-up.

Automatic Audio Vs. Setting Audio Manually

Recording audio on automatic adjusts all the levels of sound to an average setting. If you're recording an interview with a stick mic or a wireless lavelier the automatic mic level will record the person's voice at an average level, but once there is a silence or a gap in the conversation the audio setting feels the need to compensate by increasing the level of the background noise to make up for this absence of sound. Once the person resumes talking or you ask the next question the background goes back down again and the audio level readjusts to the voice of the person speaking. The end result is audio that is constantly going up and down. This varies between camera brands and even between individual cameras.

Even though you've set the audio to "automatic" there's no guarantee that it's going to come out sounding right. It's fine for when you're getting started. My first few weeks in the business I recorded everything on "automatic"—the audio and the automatic iris for exposure when shooting. But as you develop into a seasoned reporter-photographer you'll start to notice how background sounds can be annoying. The audio recorded on "auto" will turn out okay—but "okay" isn't good enough to make your stories stand out. Every story you go out on could be a potential entry on your resume reel, or to post to your website, so your sound has to be flawless. The audio of the interviews, the natural sound and the reporter track should all be crystal clear and require no effort to understand.

By manually setting your audio levels you can eliminate a great deal of background activity from your interview audio, making the sound much cleaner and more refined.

Be A No-Excuse MMJ—Invest In Yourself

"My tape would look a lot better if my school didn't have such crappy cameras."

"I know the sound isn't that great, but they were the only mics we had."

"The tripods we had were so clunky, I could never get the shots I wanted."

I hear this from students about their campus broadcast departments and from new MMJs all the time about having to work with gear that's cheap and clunky or that's old and been knocked around. They're legitimate gripes, but this is what's called, "Paying your dues." You're getting experience and have to learn how to overcome these hurdles in order to climb up the rungs of the ladder to a better station in a bigger market.

News directors don't want to hear excuses about why stories look or sound like crap. They've heard it all and they don't respond sympathetically to whining. You have to show them how you can **adapt and improvise** to overcome adversity.

The most direct solution is with your credit card.

If you've already invested a couple years of your life into getting a college degree at a significant financial investment, then it's time to dig a little deeper into your pockets and invest in some gear that will help your talents to stand out—a small camera, a mic, a tripod and some editing software. It'll be a few thousand dollars, but if you genuinely want to get a career in this business it should be worth it.

The same thing goes for people starting out in that first cubbyhole of a newsroom or bureau. If having a better mic or tripod is going to make a difference in the quality of your stories—*then buy it.*

At my first job I had a tripod with a pan head that was too small for the weight of the camera. The aluminum legs wobbled and the tension gears were stripped. I always had to keep a hand on the pan arm or else the camera would slowly tilt upwards and the weight of the camera would ultimately tip the tripod and go crashing to the ground. As a result, I only used it reluctantly and handheld the camera most of the time. The dilemma was that the stories that won awards were usually shot entirely on a tripod.

So I took out a loan against my car and bought a $2,500 Sachtler tripod. My co-workers thought I was nuts, but having made that investment I was committed to using my tripod *all the time.*

Once I had a great tripod to work with I aggressively started digging up stories that I could shoot on my own time, so that I wouldn't be under the constraints of daily deadlines, so I could showcase my photography and storytelling ability. Within a few short months I had an entirely new photographer's reel and awards for photography soon followed.

It wasn't the tripod that made me a better photographer. If I didn't have a decent eye to begin with, no piece of equipment on earth could have saved me. The tripod was just a tool—but it was a *better* tool. I could work faster, easier and not have to struggle.

Two years later, after I'd made the move to KCRA-TV in Sacramento, which was a direct result of the photography awards I'd accumulated, I sold that Sachtler tripod to an independent filmmaker in San Francisco for $1,800. Considering what I'd gotten out of it all, it was one of the best investments I ever made.

Invest in yourself. You can always resell it later on eBay.

THE ART OF THE INTERVIEW

KCRA reporter Tom DuHain interviews UC Davis *Chief* of *Police* Annette Spicuzza prior to a live shot.

KCRA reporter Danielle Leigh interviews a last-minute Christmas Eve shopper.

MOS—Man-On-The Street Interview

MAN-ON-THE-STREET INTERVIEWS, or **MOS**—"Get some MOS's"—are when you go up to complete strangers and ask for their opinions or reactions to something. I've found that a good rule of thumb is to approach everyone in the same way that you'd want someone with a camera and a microphone to come up to you. Be professional, courteous, relaxed, sympathetic and, whenever possible, smile.

When I go up to someone on the street I'll say, "Hi, I'm with Channel Three News. May I talk to you about what you think of all this?" It's very clear from the camera on my shoulder and the microphone in my hand that I'm asking for an on-camera interview, although, I specifically never say the word "interview" because I don't want to sound too formal and scare them off. I keep it casual, "May I talk to you about this?" Or, "May I ask you about that?"

The vast majority of VOs and VO-SOTs are of scheduled events, like a charity walkathon or parents protesting the closing of a school, events where everybody's there for the same purpose. You just need to ask two or three general questions about why people are there, what their concerns are and what the benefits or detractors of the situation are.

Every situation is different, of course. When pulling up at a house fire where neighbors are watching firefighters attack the blaze, people may spontaneously start talking to me because I've got a TV camera on my shoulder, "Oh my God, I couldn't believe how fast that place went up!"

In those cases I keep the camera rolling and just grab what they're saying. The sound should be pretty good right off the camera's shotgun microphone. Then I'll do a follow-up, with the stick mic if it's handy, keeping everything casual and off-the-cuff. "Yeah, can you tell me how you found out about this? How did this all start?" Usually people will just keep on talking.

Three Questions Will Do It

The first time new interns ride along with me they'll be scouring the press releases and scribbling down lists of questions to ask in their fresh, new reporter's notebooks. "Put your notepad away," I tell them. For the vast majority of situations, three questions are all you need.

- A General Question: "What's going on here?" "What can you tell me about this?" "What happened here?"
- A More Direct or Personal Question as to the person's reaction or how it effects them: "Why did you want to be here?" "Did you see or hear anything?" "What do you make of all this?" "Do you think this is something that people should be aware of?"
- Something Challenging or Left-Field, a question that poses a different slant on the situation without being confrontational: "It looks like there's a lot of stuff happening here, but in the grand scheme of things, do you think anybody's going to remember this tomorrow?" "Let me play devil's advocate for a moment. Everyone here is so excited, but do you think any of this is going to matter to the folks at home?" "I think everybody would agree that this is a great idea, but where's the money going to come from?"

Just a few short questions, being polite and professional, without giving anybody a reason to dislike me.

"Thanks for talking to me. May I ask your name, please?"

"Cathy Johnson." Never assume the spelling. Everybody's name is spelled differently these days.

"Is that Cathy with a 'C' or a 'K'?" And do the same with their last name. "And regular spelling for Johnson?"

Sometimes they'll respond, "What do you need that for?"

"Because we always like to credit the names of the people we talk to." After which they usually give me the spelling. Once in a while someone will say they'd rather not give their name and that's okay, too—but I've got their sound on tape.

Then I'll say, "Thank you very much for talking to me. Thanks for your time."

Always have a business card ready to hand out.

Avoid talking to any one person too much. Try to talk to as many different people as possible to gather different points of view. You don't want everybody saying the same thing. You also don't want everybody to look the same. Talk to men, women, young, old, different ethnicities, those who have money, those who don't.

Get The Names *After* The Interview

I cannot tell you how many times I've been at a scene where people are spontaneously bubbling with emotion, "Oh, my gosh, did you just see that? The man was just standing there and—"

"Well, let us talk to you," the reporter will say, raising up the mic.

"Yeah—I was just standing here and this guy just—"

"What's your name?"

"What?"

"What's your name?"

"I'm Suzy Parker—and this guy just—"

"How do you spell that? S-u-s-"

"Suzy Parker—S-u-z-y—Parker—P-a-r-k-e-r. And this guy—"

"Where are you from, Suzy? What part of town?"

"I'm from Crestwood, out in the county. So what do you want to ask me?"

"Okay, Suzy. So what did you just see?"

By that time the reporter has killed the moment. The person will start talking in a tone duller than dish water. "Well, I was just standing here, on my way to lunch when I observed a man..." All the life and fire that was there has been extinguished.

The person's words would have been so much more powerful if the mic had been simply held out and the person was asked, "I'm sorry—what were you saying? What did you see?" Just allow the person to keep on talking on their own with little interference.

It's disconcerting for a perfect stranger to be asked right off the bat for their name, how to spell it and where they live. Ask the questions first, *then* ask for their name and spelling after you've earned their trust. And never use the phrase, "Where do you live?" The response can frequently be, "Why do you need to know that?" Keep everything low-key and conversational, "And where's home, Suzy?"

Every now and then when I go up to a woman to ask an MOS question she'll respond, "Oh no, not me—I don't look good today." Or, "Oh no, I just rushed out of the house without my makeup."

I always reply, "But you look great."

Quite often the woman will relent and talk to me on-camera after all. It just gets down to making them less self-conscious and putting them at ease.

No matter what, whenever a woman says "I don't look good today"—*Do Not Agree With Her!*

The Formal Sit-Down Interview

When setting up a story on the phone be sure to specify up front that you want to do an "on-camera interview." Be very clear about this. You don't want to drive all the way there only to have the person look at you with your camera and say, "Oh, I didn't know you wanted to put me on camera. I thought this was just to get some information. I don't what to be on TV." Many people think TV stories take days to put together and not simply a matter of hours.

No Talking Until The Camera's Rolling

I strive to use as little gear as possible. Usually I only bring the camera, a tripod and a wireless lavelier microphone, which I carry in a pocket. The more gear you have, the more imposing you are. With less gear, people are more at ease. I shoot almost everything using existing light as much as possible. If the location interior is too dark, I'll go back to the car and grab a light, but this doesn't happen often.

Upon arrival at an interview location, typically an office or home, there are greetings and casual introductions and I thank the person for their time. Quite often they may start talking about their story, which is the reason why I'm there. If so, I politely intercede, "Excuse me, I'm sorry, but could we please wait a minute until I can put a microphone on you? I find that most people always say things best the first time."

I'll put the camera down and take out the wireless lav mic. "If you wouldn't mind slipping this on." I hand the person the wireless transmitter body pack. "Just drop this into a pocket or hook it to the top of your slacks, then if you'd run this," I indicate the tiny microphone with a tie-clip at the end of a thin cable, "up under your top and I'll clip it to your collar."

If this is a woman I'll turn my back while she does this.

Then the person will be trying to figure out how to clip the microphone to their shirt, invariably clipping it upside down.

"That's okay, I'll take care of this part."

As I'm clipping the mic to their collar they'll often say, "Okay, so tell me what questions you're going to ask me."

"Oh, just real simple stuff. We'll start with last year's taxes." This usually breaks the ice.

By now I will have quickly surveyed the location, chosen a place where the lighting is even and the background isn't too bright. I'll set the camera up on a tripod, grab a white balance, frame up on the person and hit the record button. If I'm working with a reporter I'll softly say, "Okay, I'm rolling."

Then I'll start, "Okay, so let's talk about. . . . "

Lighting Formal Sit-Down Interviews

If I need to use a light I keep it simple and usually just use one.

I don't set up the light so that the naked bulb is shining directly into the interviewee's eyes, blinding them. I start with the light pointed up before I turn it on. I may shoot the interview this way, bouncing a strong light up off the ceiling, giving a soft, even look without any shadows. Or I may clip some diffusion material, **scrim**, over the front barn doors of the light, then slowly tilt the lamp down towards the person being interviewed.

I always encourage shooters to see what it's like being on the receiving end of the lighting. If it's too bright and you're wincing or squinting, then adjust the light until it is easier on the eyes. You should always strive to make the person in front of the camera as comfortable as possible.

Set the camera up on a tripod and frame up. Avoid having the interviewee seated against a bright background or being too close to a flat wall so they come out looking like a prison mug shot.

If I'm going to be sitting off to the side of the camera and not actually looking through the viewfinder, I'll frame the interviewee in a medium or medium-close shot so that if they shift in their chair they won't lean out of the frame.

Conducting A Sit-Down Interview

Unlike grabbing an MOS from a complete stranger, the sit-down interview has been set up ahead of time so the questions tend to be more specific and involved, lasting anywhere from five to ten minutes. It can run longer if you're working on a series or long-form piece. For a same-day story anything beyond that is a waste, eating up time to log and shooting lots of material you're never going to be able to use.

Even in this situation, I tend to start off with the big broad question, "So tell me about this?" No doubt the interviewee has been mulling over what they've been planning to say anyway and this gives them a chance to get this out.

From there I start digging deeper, depending on how in-depth their initial response was and what the subject of the story is. I may wrap up with a left-field question or a polite challenge question just to see what their response might be to an opposing point of view. Since the interview is being conducted on their turf I don't want to be rude, so I'll couch this with a smile and say, "Okay, last question. And please allow me to play devil's advocate here." By politely alerting them that I'm now going to ask a challenging question, the moment is diffused and the interviewee doesn't take offense, as they could if I was throwing them a curve ball or being confrontational.

Never Take Notes During An Interview

The instant a reporter starts scribbling in a notepad during an interview the person they're talking to starts looking suspicious and their eyes start glancing down at the notepad, trying to see what is being written about them. The reporter, of course, doesn't realize this because they're looking down at what they're writing.

Any notes that need to be jotted down should be written afterwards.

Look Them Right In The Eyes

Whether you're doing a quick MOS or a formal sit down interview, always maintain direct eye contact with the person you're talking to. Never look away. Keep your mouth shut and quietly nod. Let the person finish talking and resist the urge to jump in too quickly with the next question. Sometimes by not saying anything for a few seconds the person feels compelled to carry on talking, occasionally saying something that you weren't expecting.

Only interject as a last resort, such as if the person starts rambling off in a different direction from the topic of conversation, and try to politely reign them back in.

People often don't know where to look when a camera is pointing at them and sometimes start off by talking directly into the camera. This is only natural, they're used to seeing people speaking into the camera on talk shows and don't know any better. I usually try to say beforehand, "And you can just look at me and don't worry about the camera." Occasionally when I don't and the person starts out answering my question and looking into the camera I just look around from the viewfinder with a smile and say, "Oh, that's okay, you can just look at me and don't worry about the camera." This puts them at ease because now they know what to do. They usually respond, "Oh, okay," and start over.

Always keep in mind that TV is personal. People watch the news at home in their living room, den, kitchen and bedroom, often with other family members. They think of the anchors, reporters and weather people as folks they know and refer to them by their first names. When going up to people out on the streets, approach them as you would your neighbors whom you've waved to a hundred times. You could be from their favorite station.

Using The Light That's There

It's called Natural Lighting, Available Lighting and Existing Lighting. I call it Beautiful.

Unless I'm shooting at night, I almost always make use of the light that's available, whether it's indoors or outside. I can count on one hand the number of times that I'll pull out a light to shoot an interview over the course of a year. This is not out of laziness, but stems from my own commitment to "keeping it real." I love the beauty of light and rather than haul out a light kit to make a place look the way that I want it to, I prefer to adapt my camera to the real light that's on hand. To me, that's the essence of journalism—to interfere as little as possible with the reality of what's already there.

Shooting Wide, Sun Over The Shoulder

Most photographers shoot interviews, MOS's and reporter stand-ups with the sun over their shoulders so that the sun is full on the subject's face.

Personally, I call this "rude lighting." It's harsh and the person is usually squinting and uncomfortable. Direct sunlight on the face also accentuates any wrinkles, blemishes and imperfections in the skin. This can make people uncomfortable and embarrassed when they see themselves on TV. I want people to be relaxed and happy with how they look.

Shooting Wide And Backlit

I take the opposite approach. I turn people around 180 degrees so that their back is to the sun and their face is in the shade. This way they have a beautiful backlight around them, separating them from the soft background.

Also, most photographers shoot their outside interviews by being up close with the lens wide, having the subject in crisp focus. Unfortunately, everything in the background is in focus as well. (This is known as "deep depth of field.")

Camera Back, Zoomed In & Backlit

If I'm shooting a formal interview outside I like to get the camera back ten, fifteen or twenty feet and zoom in. I also dial up the shutter speed so that the iris, or F-stop, is at the widest opening so that there is a very small area of the picture that is in focus. (This is called "eliminating the depth of field.") This allows me to be focused exclusively on the person being interviewed and throws everything in the background out of focus. This eliminates distracting backgrounds like hard lines from doors, walls or windows that are behind the person's head, as well as address numbers on buildings, signs and billboards that might be a distraction.

Actual frame blow-ups from an interview with cancer survivor Ruben Gonzalez, shot on Sony XDCAM.

Also, should somebody walk by in the background and wave into the camera, they will be so out of focus that no one will be able to make out anything they are doing.

Lavelier "Lav" Microphone Placement

Wrong—

There's an old adage, "Microphones are meant to be heard and not seen."

If the mic is clipped to the front of the interviewee's shirt and the black cable is seen running down the front of their clothing, that's the sign of a journalist who's either new to the business or who just doesn't care.

Right—

Run the cable up the inside of an interviewee's shirt or jacket or around from behind and conceal the cable behind their collar.

The cable is then looped and clipped on the inside of the blouse or collar. This will keep the cable from dangling out and showing in the shot.

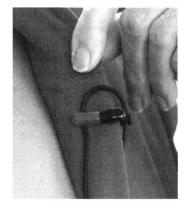

Delicate Situations—Mic'ing A Woman

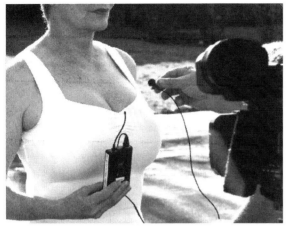

Almost every day a TV news photographer faces a sensitive situation when clipping a lavelier microphone to someone for an interview. When it's a member of the opposite sex it's particularly necessary to display professionalism and tact.

When I got into the business it had never occurred to me that I would have to clip a mic onto a woman's blouse in direct proximity to her breasts. It sounds funny, but this comes up several times in a week and you have to quickly learn how to do this in a way that is neither embarrassing to you or to the woman about to be interviewed.

It's best to do this quickly and directly. I avoid looking the woman in the eye and also make a point not to allow my eyes to roam in any way towards her breasts. I tend to focus on the area of the chest just above the breasts and below the neck as the ideal spot to clip the microphone.

"Excuse me, I'm just going to clip this right here." If she is wearing a T-shirt type of top where there is no easy collar to clip a mic to I'll say, "Excuse me, I'm just going to pinch a little piece of your shirt right here." Or, "Could you just pinch a bit of your shirt right there?" Then clip the mic there.

Every now and then a woman will joke, "I bet you love your job, don't you?" Or when a woman is running the mic up the inside of her blouse, she might say, "I thought you were supposed to be doing this part." When this happens I make a point to never respond verbally, but simply make a little smile, acknowledging the joke, and look away.

It's important that you never follow up a joke like that with another joke referring to the female body. You never know how a woman is going to react and the last thing you want is to return to the station and discover the news director wants to talk to you about a phone call he'd received from a woman you'd shot an interview with. This has never happened to me, but I can attest that it happens.

WRITING

A newspaper story is written to be read.

A TV news story is written to be spoken.

A newspaper story length is determined by word count.

In TV news, we count the seconds.

Ninety percent of what we cover doesn't matter to 90% of the viewers. Ninety percent of what we cover might matter to 10% of the viewers—if you're lucky. The test in this business is to try to make something interesting and relevant to people who have no vested interest. That's where the storytelling comes in. That's where you characterize a person not as a role player but as a real person. You put in backstories, you put in motivations, you ask questions that draw stuff out. This whole thing on universal appeal is kind of a breakthrough in getting people to understand that you're not just cramming facts—*you're telling a story with the facts.*
Wayne Freedman, KGO-TV, San Francisco

—

A lot of reporters go at it backwards. They get all the facts and they figure out how they're going to put the facts into a story. I look at the story and I put the facts in. You don't make the story fit the facts—you find the story first. The facts will fall into place if you find a good story.

There are three timelines in a story. The first is the events as they happen. The second timeline is how you shot them. The third timeline, and the most important, is how you put the first two timelines together. And that's where your true fun comes in—as long as you stay true to the subject. You could take the ending and put it at the beginning, move stuff around. That's where you structure and that's where you build the piece.

The idea that there's more than a linear timeline boggles the mind of people. The idea that you could take classic forms of literature and structure and apply them to a television news story isn't liberating to them. A story can have a prologue and be bookended. You can bookend in the present and go back in the past and tell what happened and come back to the present. Flashbacks, all this stuff. They don't think that way.

Wayne Freedman, KGO-TV, San Francisco

I BELIEVE THAT THE BEST TV NEWS WRITING works on the same principle as a well-told joke—use as few words as possible in the setup and get to the punch line. Simple, direct, to the point. Focus on the facts and spare the artful prose.

Everything I know about news writing has been learned on-the-job, working from reporters' scripts, editing to the rhythms of their words, and trying my own hand. Of course, *thinking* that you can write and actually *writing* are two different things. There is no greater test once you've written your first news script than to try reading it out loud without getting tongue-tied.

My goal is to tell the folks watching at home about something they didn't know before, and tell it in a way that is fresh and engaging. I want the viewer to be involved and care about what they're watching, and then feel better for having seen the story.

While I work in TV news every day, I don't get the opportunity to report every day. For that reason I encourage you to get Wayne Freedman's *It Takes More Than Good Looks to Succeed at Television News Reporting, 2nd Edition*. Wayne was interviewed earlier in this book and is a working reporter who's been pounding the pavement every day for over three decades. His life is storytelling and his perspectives into the art and craft of writing compelling and unique television news stories will provide great insight for you in developing your own storytelling talents.

The next book I believe you should keep close is the dictionary. Nothing reflects bad writing worse than bad spelling, compounded with the improper use of words such as "to" and "too," and "they're," "there" and "their." In this day and age of the Internet where everything is written, it is impressive to a potential employer to be able to write properly.

A note on the stories that I will be presenting in the coming pages. None of them are award-winners, and that is intentional. These are same-day stories. The type of assignments that you as reporters could be sent out to cover on any given day. Stories about people and what they do, and for those reasons alone they are of value.

TRT—Total Running Time

One of the first facts-of-life you learn in TV news is how long a story can run. The average running time of a local TV news story in the 1980s was 1:45. A story was self-contained with all the information told in a package that had a solid beginning, middle and end. By the 1990s a package was 1:30, or "a buck thirty." By 2010 it had been condensed even more to 1:15. Going from 105 seconds down to 75 seconds' time to tell the same story.

With shorter running times a package is now looked upon less as the whole story and more as part of the flow of information in a newscast.

Ashleigh Walters in a live truck, writing a story on a deadline.

USA Today took its cue from TV news by making newspaper stories short and quick to read. Ironically, TV stations are now taking cues from *USA Today*.

You have to learn how to count the calories of a story. Whatever you don't absolutely *have* to have gets cut right off the top. TV news is all about time and using the seconds you have as efficiently and effectively as you can.

- Keep it fast.
- Keep it moving.
- Keep the viewers from flipping the channel.

You Never Know What You're Going To Get

So much of the news business is running by the seat of your pants, purely improvisational. Once you leave the station you never know exactly what you're going to do or what you're going to get. You have no idea what it's going to be like until you get there. You put questions to people you've never met before, with no idea what they're going to say. You're filming events that you can't control, where anything can happen. Often your job is little more than driving someplace and just going with the flow until you've got enough sound bites and footage to put together your "buck-fifteen." Sometimes that requires rolling until there's an hour's worth of footage. Other times you get everything you need in just seven or eight minutes of material.

Then the first thought that shoots into your head is, "My God, what am I going to do with this stuff?" This is why writing can frequently be the most time-consuming element in the journalist's process. It's the point when everything that's been acquired—press releases, research material, written notes, your interviews, ideas for the anchor intros and for your script—has to be distilled into a written script that will time out, on average, to seventy-five to eighty seconds of television. And it doesn't matter whether you're working with eight minutes of footage or eighty minutes—it all has to fit into that :75-:80 TRT.

KCRA reporter Chris Riva writing a story for the KCRA.COM website from the press room of the San Francisco 49ers training camp during the final playoffs to the Super Bowl in 2012.

Write Your Own Intros

Once I've finished shooting the story and am loading the gear back into the car for the drive back to the station, my mind shifts into the writing mode and how I'm going to tell the story. My very first thought is always, "Where do I start?"

Every news story starts with an "intro," when one or both of the anchors reads an introduction to the story of two or three sentences to set up the story. This needs to be easygoing and conversational so that it flows effortlessly from the anchors' lips. And it needs to have a "hook"— something intriguing to grab the viewers' attention.

Some reporters write their script first and think up the intro afterword, as if the intro and the story are two separate things. For myself, I think of the intro and the package as being the same thing. I regard the intro as a springboard which will launch the viewer into the story.

When trying to come up with the intro, I think what the story is about in a broad, big picture sense, then ask myself, "What could we start off saying that would grab people, make them curious, touch a chord with their own lives to make them want to watch?" And also, "What does an audience need to know about this story in order to get into it and understand it?"

```
ANCHOR INTRO:
It's been a strange year weather-wise, with
rains late into the summer. For some
businesses, like construction companies, this
has been bad—but for others, like winemakers,
it has been golden. KCRA 3's Mike Carroll
shows us why this season's grape harvest could
be the best in decades.
```

This intro begins with a reference to the weather, which everyone can relate to, then segues into businesses that are suffering, while an entirely different type of business stands to thrive—painting a picture of winners and losers, conflict and drama. With the stage set, the story can now begin.

When I get back to the station the first thing I'll do is go to the producer. "So, Mike, what have you got for me?" I try to hit the producer with my "hook." If the producer responds, "Okay, I'll buy that," then I'm off to the races. And usually a producer won't ask anything else about the story until I submit a script.

This works much more effectively than if I'd said, "This is a really cool story," and start rolling off a litany of facts and what my pictures are and blah-blah-blah—making it sound like I haven't figured out the story yet. Producers *hate* having to hold a reporter's hand. It's perceived as weakness, that you're in over your head and not capable of doing your job. Producers have their hands full as it is with writing and organizing their show, so they don't need to be figuring out your story for you. The producer could start mapping out how they want the story to go, then the story becomes their story and not the story you wanted to tell.

Always be in control of your stories. The more authority you exercise in telling your stories and the more self-confidence you are able to convey to the assignment desk and the producers, the more likely they will be to leave you alone.

> Producers will almost always edit your intro to make it shorter. However, if you write it cleverly they're less likely to change it too much.

> **Bottom Line:** When you write a story, write *everything*—the intro, the script, and the tag. Don't let other people put **their** words into **your** story.

Edit Your Scripts *Yourself*

It's one thing to write your scripts long and then edit them down to time. Just be sure to edit them down yourself. Producers get very irritated with people who consistently write long scripts and whine, "I don't know what to cut." Doing the writing is *your* job.

When my scripts time out to 1:45 in the computer I always say to the producer, "I know it's too long, but I'll cut it down in the editing." As long as I always turn in a finished story that runs 1:15 or 1:20, and don't try to sneak through a 1:35, producers trust me and leave me alone.

Writing Styles—Information And Reaction

This is a type of story that a lot of reporters will do when facing tight deadlines. It consists of the reporter telling the information of the event and punctuating it with quick bites of people reacting to it.

Example: Covering a snowstorm—the reporter track provides the details of the storm and weather conditions, where the storm is hitting the hardest and what's being done to keep the roads clear. This would be broken up with quick four to eight second bites of people saying what the road conditions are like, how cold and hard the wind is on their face or how the storm is more intense than they had expected. The bites don't include information or facts about the storm, simply their own reactions to it.

It's a quick, efficient way of getting the story on the air for times when the reporter must literally write the script while on the road because there's not going to be any time to review the footage before it's time to start editing to "make air."

Shooting a story on my day off and with my own Canon 7D DSLR camera about independent filmmakers in Sacramento.

Doing Stories On Your Own Time

You're going to come across stories that you'd really like to do—and which would also be fantastic on your reel. The problem is that to do them properly will require several hours, if not a whole day, or may even need to be shot a few hours here and there over time. There's no way an assignment desk is going to cut you loose to do that. Daily news is a beast that constantly needs to be fed. In the case of smaller, entry-level newsrooms, the newscasts have to be filled by even smaller staffs who are kept running around, gathering stories all the time. This is just a TV fact-of-life and it's never going to change, no matter what level market you get up to. Even now, after being in the business for three decades, I still periodically shoot something that I really want to do on a day off—on my own time.

Some people take the view that doing a story in their spare time is working for free, that they've done enough unpaid work during their internship and now that they're working in a newsroom everything they do should be "on the clock." I take the view that it's so hard to get into this business, and there are so many people who'd love to do what we do, that occasionally doing a story that matters to you on your own time is an extension of "paying your dues."

For me, these stories are why I wanted to do this type of work in the first place. While they take time out of my personal life, they're also personally rewarding and keep me going through the times when I'm stuck out in pouring rain or 100 degree heat all day.

Of the four or five stories on the audition reel that got me a job at KCRA, half were shot and edited on my own time. Since I was under no time constraints to get them completed I was able to take the time to make them exactly the way I wanted. Each of those stories went on to win numerous awards, which also didn't look bad on my resume. It's worth noting that the salary that came with the new job was more than double what I was earning before, so the extra time and effort more than paid off.

One story that I produced on my own time was a profile of an artist who did intricate photo-collage art that took months to create. I'd meet up with her for an hour or two every couple of weeks, documenting her process. I later interviewed her using multiple cameras and many different angles, resulting in hours of footage, which took me weeks to edit into a story that ultimately ran four and a half minutes long. Not the type of piece that can run on a regular news day. So I saved it and pitched it to a producer to run on New Year's Day when the staffing is low due to vacations and typically not a lot of news going on. A long story like this would fill a large chunk of her show and also give her a unique story that she could promote throughout the newscast.

"The only thing I want, if you choose to run it, is that—since I've done all of this on my own time—I don't want it cut it down for time. I want it to run as-is."

The producer took a deep breath. "That's an awfully long story for me to run. Let me take a look at it and I'll get back to you."

I gave her the tape and later in the day she came back to me.

"Okay, here's the deal. I'll run it exactly as it is. But you have to promise me that you won't tell any of the other producers or managers about it or else they'll want to run it. I want to save it for my show."

"Done."

The story ran on New Year's Day in its entirety. The producer got compliments for how good the newscast looked on a holiday, and I got a lot of compliments for how original the story was. One of the managers even called me into his office and pitched me on doing another piece just like it on a story idea he had. Then I asked, "So when are you looking at running this?"

"Tonight at six o'clock."

"Tonight? You do realize that the story I did that ran last night was something that I've been working on for over three months. There's no way I could do anything like what you have in mind in just a matter of six or seven hours."

I always say that most folks have no idea how long or how quickly it can take for TV people to do their work. That can even hold true for some people in TV.

My First Reporter-Photographer Package

Before KWCH-TV in Wichita, Kansas, had been purchased by new owners in the early '80's and started the expansion that allowed me to break into the business, all the reporters had to work double-duty as both reporters and photographers. I loved picking the brains of the reporters about how they could do both jobs, which they were happy not to have to do any more because of how heavy and bulky the gear was, and they'd always close by saying, "My stuff didn't look that good." I once pulled a library tape out of the archives to check out what some of their stories looked like and, frankly, they were right—they didn't look very good. But then, neither did my stuff at that time.

Still, the idea of shooting and writing a story was stuck in my head. I thought back to my friend Mike Dieffenbach and his stories back in St. Louis. I've always enjoyed putting words together and, when I was younger, had ambitions of being a writer. Combining these two passions into putting together a story entirely on my own—*my* way—was something I had to take a stab at. Besides, a TV script is only a page or so long, so even if it took me a few hours to write, I should be able to come up with *something*.

By fall of 1984, I'd been at KWCH for nearly a year, working Tuesdays through Saturdays[3]. On weekends we typically had one reporter and two photographers for dayside and the same for nightside. This arrangement still holds true for most newsrooms across the country.

A reporter and a photographer would team up to cover the lead story of the day while the second photographer would run around town on "VO Patrol," picking up VO's and VO-SOTs. The other shooters hated VO Patrol, but I preferred it. I'd be handed a stack of five to seven sheets of paper, each with an assignment, location and start—the opening of a new park or library, a neighborhood cleanup, a chili cook off, a car wash

---

[3] Ironically, this is still my shift almost thirty years later, even at a different station 2,000 miles away.

fundraiser—and twenty minutes of a college football or basketball game for the sports department. I'd also have to be available for any breaking news during the day—a fire, a shooting, a drowning, etc. For me, this was a challenge. "How fast can I shoot this?"

Earlier that year I'd been to the N.P.P.A. Workshop in Norman, Oklahoma, and returned with a clearer sense of purpose. Every week I was becoming a better photographer and a more professional newsman. Most of all, I was becoming more confident in myself and what I could do. I worked at collaborating more closely with the reporters on stories, but at the end of the day, it was the person who wrote the script and tagged it out with their name ("Julie Becker, KWCH, Wichita") who determined how a story was going to be told. I came to realize that the only way to have authorship over my pictures and sound would be for me to tell the stories myself—as both the photographer *and* the reporter.

Two of the instructors at the Workshop who made big impressions on me were Larry Hatteburg, who was also based in Wichita at KAKE-TV, and Darrel Barton, who had once worked for Hatteburg at KAKE before heading back to his hometown of Oklahoma City and KFOR-TV. Both had been one-man band reporter-photographers and both had been N.P.P.A. Photographers of the Year. Their work inspired me to want to try this myself even more.

When I was out on VO Patrol, I'd select one story that I thought had the potential to be more than just a thirty-second reader, and shoot a little more footage and a few extra interviews. When I'd get back to the station I'd take the initiative to expand these thirty-second VO-SOTs into full packages, writing up the scripts, which the weekend anchor-producer would voice and I would edit. This became my news writing training ground.

This is all to explain how, one year after having learned how to turn a TV news camera on, I embarked on doing my first on-air reporter-photographer package.

In fall of 1984 KWCH reporter Julie Becker became the weekend anchor-producer. Wichita being a smaller market, the weekend anchor was also responsible for writing and producing the newscasts. On the first Saturday that Julie was anchoring I had an unusual early morning assignment. In the downtown river area was a sizeable duck population and one of the ducks had been spotted with a large dart lodged in its neck from someone who'd shot it. Volunteers from animal control and the SPCA were going out to the river early in the morning to try to capture the duck so it could be treated. I got there early and spent an hour or so with them while they searched for the duck, getting lots of great shots and natural sound of their failed efforts to capture the duck, as well as interviews with the volunteers afterward. Then I went on with the rest of the Saturday VO patrol, shooting half a dozen assignments around town before getting back to the station.

Julie, our new weekend anchor-producer, already looked slightly overwhelmed by all the work before her so I offered to take a few minutes of the newscast off her hands. I told her about the duck story and how it would make a great package, then I said that I'd be willing to write it and turn it into a package, provided I could track it myself.

Julie chewed on that for a moment, considering that this was her first day helming the weekend shows, and knowing full well that if my package stunk she would be the person who'd take the heat for putting it on the air. At the same time, I could see the wheels turning in her head. A half-hour news show boiled down to about twenty-two minutes of news, minus breaks for commercials. Then deduct weather and sports and she was left with twelve minutes of each newscast that she had to fill. My package would come in at 1:45, plus a twenty-second intro and a fifteen-second tag. That added up to 2:20 of news, or one-sixth of a newscast that I was handing her and that she didn't have to deal with. Finally, Julie shrugged, "Okay," then went back to writing up the dozen or so scripts that she was already behind on.

I isolated myself in an edit bay and logged all the interviews in detail, as well as notating the best shots with the cleanest natural sound. Then I rolled a sheet of paper into the carriage of a typewriter. My chest started to knot up and a wave of terror washed over me. "What am I doing? Who am I fooling? Why am I doing this?" But there's one thing about writing news—there's no time for writer's block.

When I was shooting the search for the wounded duck, I had already predetermined that I wanted to tell the story in chronological order. Using that concept as my guide, I scanned through the tape log, picked out a couple pieces of natural sound of the search, then added one of the interview bites from one of the rescuers expressing their concerns.

"Okay, that's good for ten seconds or so," I thought to myself. "Time to write some track and explain to the folks at home what's going on."

Most packages are made up of paragraphs of reporter tracks that are broken up by three to five short bites. I wanted to go the opposite route. I wanted to keep my tracks short and let the pictures, sound and interviews show and tell what happened. As much as possible, I only wrote a line or two of track when it was necessary to provide information or connect bites and video.

I gave my script to Julie to read and review. Much to my surprise, she approved it without changing a single word. I then went directly into the audio booth to record the voice track. This proved to be my biggest hurdle. I *hated* the sound of my own voice. (This was back in the time before everybody had camcorders and had grown up seeing what they looked and sounded like.) Up to this moment, I don't think I'd ever heard what my voice sounded like.

"That's me? That can't be. That's not what I sound like."

I also discovered that I tended to slur words together. I had to reach down into a lower register and project like an actor on stage. I had to belt it out. I tracked and re-tracked my words, over and over, take after take, forcing myself to enunciate more clearly and punch up my voice to make it more dynamic.

I also did a lot of rewriting in the audio booth. It's one thing to write a sentence, it's something entirely different to read it out loud. I found that there are some words that don't flow as easily off of my lips as others. Audio tracks need to be smooth and conversational and easy.

> I'll never forget watching my news director Steve Ramsey, at KWCH in Wichita, coaching a new reporter and saying, "Don't write a story—*tell* a story. And don't be afraid to over exaggerate. Make your words bigger, stronger. Belt it out to me. *Command* me to listen."

The editing was not that difficult, especially since I was simply editing one shot, then shuttling ahead to find the next shot, and then the next, as opposed to shuttling back and forth on the tape looking for shots. Although, I did take more time to make the editing as precise as possible since this was, after all, my debut reporter piece.

Later, when the story aired, I couldn't help but notice that Julie couldn't conceal a little crook of a smile as she introduced the story and said my name. Other photographers had done photo-essays with music and natural sound pieces, but this was the first time that any of the photographers—with the sole exception of chief photographer Jim Anderson, who'd been originally hired as a reporter-photographer—had reported, written and tracked their own story as a reporter.

The story ran without a hitch. As I was driving home that night to begin my weekend, I was proud of my story and what I'd done, taking the initiative to push myself to another level as a photojournalist. But then I started to think again. I'd done this entirely on my own. I hadn't gotten any prior approval from management to do a story on my own and tag them out as a reporter. Maybe the other photographers hadn't done this before for a reason? Maybe there's a management policy regarding this? What will the reporters think? I could be treading on their turf. Maybe I should have run this by somebody first? It was the beginning of a long string of second thoughts and questions that swirled around in my head over that weekend.

Everything seemed normal when I came back into work on Tuesday. In fact, everything seemed great. Everybody that I passed as I came in, both photographers and reporters and producers said, "Hey, Mike. Great story." Or, "Great job on the duck." In fact, it seemed almost too positive. "This is too much," I began to wonder. "Am I being set up for something?"

I got into the photographers' lounge and editing room where the special projects photographer was busy cutting a feature. He swung around and said, "So what'd you think of the note?"

"Note?"

"Yeah, the note Steve Ramsey put up in the newsroom about your duck story."

"I didn't know about a note."

"It's tacked up on the bulletin outside his office."

"Crap," I suddenly thought to myself. "There *was* a reason why none of the other shooters had done their own packages before, and now I'm about to have the book thrown at me."

I went into the newsroom and as I walked across I could see a page of KWCH letterhead tacked dead center on the bulletin board. The note had the heading, "Carroll's Duck":

This was known as an "atta boy." Getting a pat on the back like that from Steve Ramsey was enough to fill up your gas tank with inspiration to do it again. After that, every Saturday I strived to turn something into a reporter package. Many of them would have been just as well off as VO-SOTs that Julie could read over. But each one was a little something extra that went to make the weekend news stand out just a little bit more. And each was another notch on the ladder of experience.

SCRIPT: Wounded Duck

I didn't keep any of the scripts from my starting-out days in Kansas. Besides, by the time I'd finished tracking them and cutting the story, the original pages were all marked over beyond recognition. This is a transcript of my first reporter-photographer story from the aircheck.

ANCHOR INTRO:
As we had been reporting to you last night, the Humane Society has been struggling to save a mallard duck along the Arkansas River who has been cruelly wounded by two blow-gun darts sticking out of his head. This morning they resumed their attempt and Mike Carroll was with them.

TAKE SOT:
It was shortly after dawn when members of the Humane Society arrived.

(snapping net into place)
There. We're all ready.

TRACK:
Ellen Koerner and Julia Rassmussen have been tracking the wounded mallard for four days now. They had hoped they might be able to capture him in his sleep.

NAT
No luck. Can't find him.

TRACK:
THE MALLARD IN QUESTION IS LIKE MOST DUCKS AROUND WICHITA'S RIVERSIDE AREA — EXCEPT THIS PARTICULAR ONE HAS TWO BLOW DARTS STICKING OUT OF HIS HEAD.

NAT
Is he out there in the pond?

TRACK
IT SEEMED LIKE IT WAS GOING TO BE
ANOTHER MORNING OF FRUSTRATION —
WHEN —

NAT
I found him. Been walking past him
all morning long.

JULIA RASMUSSEN, VOLUNTEER
I just turned around and looked over
there and saw the orange and just —
I just — there he was.

TRACK
NOW THE ONLY PROBLEM WAS TO CATCH
HIM.

NAT
(They attempt to catch duck with
net. Duck flies away)
He was right there! Oh!

TRACK
EVEN THE FISH AND GAME DEPARTMENT
SHOWED UP WITH A BIRD DOG TO HELP
WITH THE RESCUE. BUT THE DUCK, AS
WELL AS BEING A GOOD FLYER, PROVED
TO BE JUST AS GOOD OF A SWIMMER.

(In video, dog is swimming toward
duck, but duck quickly swims away.)

NAT
He's coming your way — right above
you. He's right above you.

(In video, man from Fish & Game
attempts to capture the duck with a
net. Again, the duck flies off into
the middle of the river.)

MAN FROM FISH & GAME
He's not in too bad of shape.

ELLEN KOERNER, WICHITA HUMANE
SOCIETY
No. See, I thought he couldn't fly
and that's when —

JULIA RASMUSSEN
That's the first time I've seen him
fly.

TRACK
SO ONCE AGAIN THEY WENT HOME EMPTY-
HANDED, TO TRY AGAIN ANOTHER DAY.

(Tight shot of duck with blow dart
in it's neck floating on the
water.)

MIKE CARROLL, EYEWITNESS NEWS,
WICHITA.

ANCHOR TAG:
A FOOTNOTE TO THAT STORY: THE
HUMANE SOCIETY SAYS TO STAY AWAY
FROM THAT DUCK BECAUSE THEY WILL
CAPTURE IT AND GIVE IT THE MEDICAL
TREATMENT THAT IT NEEDS AND THAT
THEY WILL TRY AGAIN TOMORROW.

SAME DAY STORY: The Bee House

WEDNESDAY, APRIL 27, 2011. 11:30 PM

I'd spent the morning in a courtroom covering a routine arraignment before returning to the station.

"Load that stuff into the system and take your lunch," Melissa on the assignment desk said, and handed over some printouts. "Then head out to Fair Oaks and check this out. Maybe it's a VO-SOT, or maybe you can turn it into one of your packages. You aren't allergic to bees, are you?"

1:30 PM

I knocked on the door of Meagan Helton, who'd sent an e-mail telling us how she and her family had moved into the Fair Oaks neighborhood the previous December, only to discover that the house directly across the street from her was abandoned and the walls had become home to tens of thousands of bees. It was now the early days of summer and the bees were becoming active. Meagan, understandably, was concerned about the safety of her children. I shot an interview with Meagan, then went out into the street to check out the bee house for myself.

The afternoon sun was behind the house and the air around it was alive with thousands of bright buzzing backlit honey bees zipping in and out of gaps in the walls. I've learned from shooting other stories involving bees that their sole purpose in life is to serve the hive—if you don't interfere with their mission, they won't bother you. With that in mind, I walked carefully up to the front door and knocked to see if anyone was in the house, but no one answered.

I went back to my car, pulled out the tripod and started shooting tight shots of the bees with the long end of the zoom lens. Gradually, I worked my way closer to the house and the places from which the bees were coming and going and was then able to see just how massive the infestation was. In the area above the garage doors some of the wood had rotted—or been *eaten* by the bees—and honeycombs were literally pushing out from the walls of the house.

To visually convey just how amazing this was I did several shots that started out wide, then quickly zoomed in to tight close-ups on the honeycombs crawling with bees. Just as I'd anticipated, the bees couldn't care less about me, so I was able to move fairly close to the house and shoot a number of super-tight close-ups of the bees crawling in and out of gaps in the walls. On a story like this, you can't have too many close-ups of bees.

After that, I loaded my tripod back in the car and went around to some of the neighboring houses, knocking on doors to see what other people on the street had to say. There was no trouble finding neighbors who shared Meagan's concerns but, unfortunately, nobody felt comfortable talking on-camera. I was lucky enough to be able to grab a quick bit of sound with a mailman, who confirmed the problems with the house, but that was it.

2:30 PM

When I'm shooting I'm always thinking about what I need to ask next and what I need to shoot next—until there's no more "next" left.

I had the interview with Meagan, a little sound from the mailman, and numerous shots of the house and the bees—eighteen minutes of footage in all. It would have been ideal to have two or three or more interviews with neighbors, but this was going to have to do. For a story that would run no more than 1:15—75 seconds—certainly there was more than enough for that.

While driving back I called the city department responsible for situations like this. They'd been working with the owner of the property, as well as with a beekeeper. Since the bee population across North America has been declining, they wanted to relocate the bees rather than call in pest control and eradicate them, but they were going to do one or the other in the next two weeks before the summer days got warmer and the bees got worse.

I then called Melissa on the assignment desk to let her know what I had and that I could easily "package it."

Writing On The Go

Some people listen to the radio or talk on their cell phones while they drive. For me, driving gets the wheels in my head turning. I'll sort through the facts of the story, trying to come up with an intro for the anchors to lead into the package. Once I have the intro worked out, it's much easier to jump right into the story.

I'll often make a list, either mentally or on paper, of the facts of the story:

- What's important?
- Why do people need to know and why should they care?
- How does it effect or impact people's lives?

At stoplights I'll scribble down what I can, or pull over and write out an intro and any sentences that I might be able to use to tie the facts of the story together. None of this will be in any particular kind of order. I may write the last line first, then work my way backwards. It doesn't matter, just whatever comes to me. By getting some of the writing done this way— and keeping both hands on the wheel—it helps me to get a head start before getting back to the station.

Logging

3 PM

In an edit bay, loading my footage into Avid. This takes around five minutes. I pulled out my scrawled notes to type up the intro. I do write in Word, constantly hitting the Save key, then copy and paste my finished script into the newsroom system for the producers to review.

Once all the footage is loaded into the computer I go through it and log the relevant interview bites. When I first started doing packages in Wichita I logged everything—interviews, natural sound, etc. Now I only log the interviews and only write down the sound that I might actually use. In the case of this story, since I only had the one interview and the bite with the mailman, this went pretty fast. I make careful notes of:

```
MAILMAN               (Who's talking)
CL 22  10.55          (Clip Number and Timecode)
I've been here on this route for five or six
years and they've been here ever since.
      (Transcription of the Sound Bite)
```

Writing

As I'm logging the sound bites I'll come up with lines of track to write into or out of the bites. Rather than run the risk of forgetting them, I'll go ahead and write these down in the log notes. This way, by the time I've finished logging I could well have a rough draft of the script and can go directly into writing new lines to connect all the pieces together into a script.

Quite often during an interview someone will mention some really good information that I'll want to use in the story, but the way they say it is too long or rambling to use as an on-camera bite. In that case, I'll paraphrase their information down into a short bit of reporter track.

I work to keep my tracks as short as possible so that I can use more bites and natural sound to tell the story, rather than a lot of me talking.

5 PM

Script is finished. I copy the script out of Word and paste it into the system for the "E.P."—the executive producer in charge of the newscasts, who reads and approves all scripts. The E.P. is looking mostly for factual errors and clarity in storytelling.

My scripts almost always time out long, 1:30 or more, so I always assure the E.P. that I'll trim the bites down once I'm cutting the story to keep it within the 1:15 TRT.

She made a minor clarification to a sentence in the script and approved it.

Editing

5:10 PM

In the audio booth to cut my track. I've gotten better at this. I've learned how my voice works and have developed a stronger reporting voice that kicks in when I get in front of the microphone. I also find that standing, rather than sitting, when recording audio tracks, helps to make for a stronger and more dynamic delivery

About half of the tracks I'm able to get in the first take. If it's a moderate to a long track I may have to do it in several bits and then butt them together in the edit room. Since I'm also the editor, I can do this much easier than a reporter who is expected to be able to deliver a whole track in one piece in order to make it easier for the editor.

5:15 PM

Hit the edit bay and started cutting. (Note: I will go into greater detail on editing in the following chapter.)

5:25 PM

All the A-roll, with my audio track and the interviews, was laid down on the Avid timeline. I do this first so I can get a running time on the story. My first edit came in at 1:35. I needed to chop out :20. I delete two interview bites and my stand-up.

5:28 PM

Started laying in the B-roll. These are the visuals of the story, the shots that go over and accompany the reporter track and the interviews. At this point, the process really picks up speed and tends to move very quickly. This last part should take ten or fifteen minutes—less if I have to.

5:45 PM

The six o'clock editing coordinator asked if I have time to cut a headline about the story for the top of the show. No problem. I cut a quick :30 of my best bee shots and "pushed"[4] them to the playback server. In the digital television station, this run is similar to sending an e-mail.

5:50 PM

Finished editing the package. Double-checked it to make sure there were no holes or other technical errors, then pushed it to the system.

---

[4] "Push"—another term for "upload." Every computer system has its own vernacular. This is what it's called in Avid.

5:51 PM

While the story is being pushed I revised the script, deleting the portions that were edited out and put in the font times of where to superimpose the location, "Fair Oaks -- :00-:05," and names of the people interviewed. In this case it was simply "Meagan Helton." into the computer system.

Then the job was done. Nothing else to do but cross my fingers, hope there won't be any glitches and everything runs smoothly. At this point, it's out of my hands.

6:00 PM

I was off the clock and cleared out of the editing bay.

This story was scheduled to run in the "B" block, right after the first commercial break, which hit at 6:10.

I'm always nervous when one of my pieces is in the news, afraid that I've missed something or there's going to be a glaring technical error. If it's running in the next few minutes I'll usually stick around to watch it.

6:12 PM

KCRA Reports at Six O'Clock returned from the commercial break to anchor Gulstan Dart speaking the words that I'd thought up just a few hours before while driving back from Fair Oaks. The story began and ran without a hitch.

Around the newsroom, producers and writers working on shows for later that evening were watching the news on the monitors they have on their desks. One producer said, "This sounds like the place down the street from my house." Then during the shots of honeycomb seeping out from the walls I heard, "Oh, Jesus, look at that!" and "Can you believe this?"

6:15 PM

The story played flawlessly. Relieved, I took up my pack and headed home.

SCRIPT: Bee House

ANCHOR INTRO:
PEOPLE ACROSS THE STATE AND AROUND
THE COUNTRY HAVE BEEN STUDYING THE
DECLINE IN BEE POPULATIONS. BUT A
FAIR OAKS WOMAN SAYS SHE MIGHT HAVE
THE ANSWER — THE ABANDONED HOUSE
ACROSS THE STREET. KCRA 2'S MIKE
CARROLL SHOWS US A HOUSE THAT HAS
THE NEIGHBORHOOD A BUZZ.

VIDEO:

Meagan Helton, Lives across from
Bee House
CL18   505-515
I moved in here in November, but it
wasn't until December that I found
out about the bees and the amount of
bees in the bee house.

"THE BEE HOUSE" — THAT'S WHAT
RESIDENTS CALL THIS HOME ON
BRICKHILL DRIVE IN FAIR OAKS.

CL18   535
Usually if it reaches over 75 or 85
degrees, that's when the swarm come
out of the hive *and they're a lot
more active.*

  ("and they're a lot more active" was trimmed for
  time.)

MEG HELTON SAYS THAT ONLY ONE OF
HER THREE CHILDREN HAS BEEN STUNG
BY THE BEES — BUT IT'S STILL EARLY
IN THE SEASON. AND HER MOTHER, WHO
FREQUENTLY HELPS OUT WITH THE
CHILDREN, IS SERIOUSLY ALLERGIC TO
BEES.

5.58
So I was just concerned for the
wellness and the well being of my
family.

(In the editing, the above sound bite
and my stand-up, which followed, was deleted for
time.)

CL49
Mike Carroll, Fair Oaks
Other residents that did not want to
go on camera said that this is not a
new situation. That the bees have
been here for years.

MAILMAN
CL 22 10.55
I've been here on this route for
five or six years and they've been
here ever since.

6.46
And from what the family has told
this company is that the bees have
been here since the 1970s.

(This sound bite was moved to replace the bite that
follows my next sentence of track. The bite that is
written into the script there was deleted due to time
constraints.)

IN FACT, LOOK AT THIS — HONEYCOMBS
ARE LITERALLY SEEPING OUT OF THE
WALLS OF THE HOUSE — IN TWO
DIFFERENT PLACES.

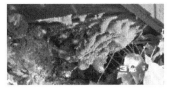

6.36
One of the bee companies that's
come out has told me that there's
at least seven different hives.

NEXT WEEK BEEKEEPERS WHO ARE GOING
TO TRY TO REMOVING THE QUEEN BEES
IN THE EFFORT TO TRANSPLANT THE
BEES TO A BETTER LOCATION, RATHER
THAN KILL THE BEES OUTRIGHT. AND
TAKE THE BUZZ OUT OF THIS NORMALLY
QUIET STREET.

IN FAIR OAKS, MIKE CARROLL, KCRA 3
REPORTS.

TAG
THE COUNTY HAS FILED VIOLATION
NOTICES ON THE PROPERTY FOR BEING
OVERGROWN, BUT SAYS THE BEES
HAVEN'T BEEN AS ISSUE BECAUSE THEY
ARE NOT DISEASE CARRIERS. THE
OWNERS OF THE HOUSE HAVE NOW HIRED
CONTRACTORS TO REMOVE THE LAVA
FAÇADE FROM THE FRONT OF THE HOUSE
TO PREVENT MORE BEES FROM CALLING
THE PLACE "HOME."

SAME DAY STORY: After-Christmas Bird Count

As I've said, news is 24/7/365. December 26, 2010, the Sunday morning after Christmas Day, I showed up at the assignment desk.

"I'm so glad you're here," the weekend morning assignment editor said. "Our dayside reporter called in sick and we're hoping that you can turn one of your reporter pieces for us today."

"Sure," I said, having no idea what the story was. "What have you got?"

"The after-Christmas bird count."

"Great. What's that?"

"People out counting birds."

"I love it."

I had no idea what I'd just agreed to. I know absolutely nothing about birds—or bird watching. One thing about news, though, is you come in to work, not knowing anything about a particular subject, but over the course of a day, meeting people and talking to them, you wind up learning something new.

"Great," she said, passing me some printouts. "Here's the e-mail I got and some contact phone numbers."

"Great. When do they start?"

"They've been out since sunrise and they'll be out all day until sunset."

"Okay, I'll give them a call."

"Oh, and we'd also like you to grab a VO-SOT of people going to the movies today. The Sunday after Christmas is one of the biggest audience attendance days at movie theaters. Just ask people why they're out and what the big movie is."

"Easy enough."

"And take a live truck, too. We'd like a live shot of traffic on the highways with people going home after the holiday."

"Will do."

I loaded into a microwave truck and quickly read over the e-mail about the bird count. At the bottom were a couple names and cell phone numbers. I called one fellow on the list, Chris Conard, who'd been out since dawn observing birds in a park very close to where I live. He said to come on down.

For twenty years I'd driven past this park in the middle of a nice neighborhood, but I never had any idea that it had a woods and a marshy area right there.

Chris was decked out in hiking pants and shirt, sunhat, binoculars and waterproof boots—a perfect visual for the story. I put a wireless microphone on him and asked him to give me a tour. As I followed him I always start out with the simplest question: "Tell me what you're doing out here?"

I spent about half an hour with Chris, following him as he wandered into the woods and marsh, occasionally hearing a bird and raising his binoculars to identify it. Then I jumped back into the truck and called another name on the list, drove up to the north part of town, met up with some more people and shot and spent some time with them.

After that I had about twenty-five minutes of footage, but not much in the way of birds. Then, on the drive to the movie theatre to shoot the VO-SOT, I came to a field with swarms of birds circling it. I pulled over and set up the camera on the tripod. Shooting with the longest end of the zoom lens, I got several minutes of nice super-tight shots of birds in flight, landing, then taking off again—just the element that I had been missing in order to illustrate the story.

I then continued on to the cinema, talked to some families about what they were going to see, then drove to a hilltop beside a highway overpass where I could set up a live shot to show the day-after-Christmas drive-home traffic. I raised the microwave mast and sent the VO-SOT footage back while I started logging the bird count story.

It was around 1:30 in the afternoon. The bird count story was scheduled to run in the six o'clock news, so I had plenty of time. However, I decided to make this a speed test—I wanted to have the story finished and fed back to the station by 3:30. This gave me two hours to log, write, get the script approved, edited and fed.

One-manning the bird count story in a live truck on an unusually warm December 26 in Sacramento. Note my ever-present MacBook, on which I wrote the story.

As soon as I started logging, one of the first things that Chris said actually sounded like a perfect bite to open the story. I went ahead and dropped that bite down onto the editing timeline. I resumed logging, found another interesting bite and put it onto the timeline as well. Then a line of track came to me that could work well coming out of Chris' opening bite and leading into the second bite, so I wrote it down into the script.

I continued logging like this, finding bites, editing them onto the timeline, writing tracks to connect the bites and explain the story—essentially editing the A-roll of the story as I went. Within an hour I had the bites picked and a script written, which I e-mailed to the producer. While waiting for script approval, and wanting to keep on track with my self-imposed deadline, I went ahead and cut my audio and started inserting my tracks in between the bites on the timeline. I had all of the A-roll completed and had started laying in the B-roll when the producer called to let me know that she'd approved my script with no changes.

Within another fifteen minutes all the B-roll had been laid down. I took a few minutes to go through and tighten up bites here and there to make the package a solid 1:15, then exported the package and fed it back.

The story helped fill the rundown of the newscast, since we were down a reporter for the day. As for my two-hour challenge—I completed it in one-hour and forty minutes.

SCRIPT: After Christmas Bird Count

INTRO:
THE DAY'S IMPROVED NICE WEATHER WAS
GREATLY APPRECIATED BY ONE GROUP OF
SACRAMENTANS — MEMBERS OF THE
SACRAMENTO AUDUBON SOCIETY — WHO
SPENT THE DAY OUTDOORS CONDUCTING AN
ANNUAL AFTER-CHRISTMAS BIRD COUNT
CENCUS OF THE AREA. KCRA 3'S MIKE
CARROLL

NATS
Cl 5   4.51
Psht. Psht, psht.

IT'S TEN IN THE MORNING AND CHRIS
CONARD IS ONLY JUST STARTING HIS
DAY.

Cl 10
There's an orange-crowned warbler.

AND CHRIS WILL BE OUT HERE IN
REICHMUTH PARK IN SOUTH SACRAMENTO
UNTIL THE SUN IS LONG GONE.

CHRIS CONARD, Audubon Bird Counter
Cl 3
1.09
Well, you can get 50 or 60 different
species of birds in this park.

CHRIS IS A PART OF THE ANNUAL AFTER-
CHRISTMAS AUDUBON SOCIETY BIRD
COUNT, WHERE MEMBERS GO OUT AND
TRACK THE VARIETY OF SPECIES AND
NUMBERS OF BIRDS IN VARIOUS PART OF
SACRAMENTO.

CHRIS
We'll often get about 150 species
throughout the entire area. It's a
circle about 15 miles across —
exactly 15 miles across.

MARK MARTUCCI
Cl 36
Did you ever find those sparrows?

MARK MARTUCCI AND DAN KOPP ARE
TRACKING THE BIRDS AROUND GARDEN
HIGHWAY.

MARK MARTUCCI
Cl 41   19.18
We break it into ten areas and then
we have sub groups and we go out and
count every bird we see.

MARK HAS SEEN HOW DEVELOPMENT IN THE
NATOMAS AREA HAS CHANGED THE TYPES
OF BIRDS HE'S SEEING — AND NOT
SEEING.

MARK MARTUCCI, Sacramento Bird Count
The burrowing owl's almost
nonexistent now where it used to be
pretty common. Development does
effect it, definitely.

MARK HAS ALSO NOTICED HOW SOME BIRDS
MOVE ON, OTHERS MOVE IN — MAKING
SACRAMENTO HOME.

IN SACRAMENTO, MIKE CARROLL, KCRA-3
REPORTS.

TAG:
THE BIRD COUNT TAKES PLACE EVERY
YEAR DURING THE FIRST WEEKEND AFTER
CHRISTMAS AND BEGAN OVER A HUNDRED
YEARS AGO AS AN ALTERNATIVE TO A
THEN AFTER-CHRISTMAS BIRD HUNTING
DAY.

LOG & SCRIPT: SPCA Adopt-A-Thon

I've made reference to logging footage and turning the log into a first draft script. In this section I'll illustrate how that process worked in creating one story.

I'm always eager to do stories with the Sacramento animal shelters to help get pets into new homes. I grew up in a home where we always had a cat and a dog. My wife Bonnie and I have two greyhounds, Alex and Ava, and are also involved in fostering greyhounds for a local rescue organization. These stories are generally easy-sells to producers because they get tremendous audience response, which is good because it translates into getting lots of pets into homes.

This story was shot quickly over the course of an hour on a Tuesday morning prior to a Sacramento SPCA (Society for the Prevention of Cruelty to Animals) adoption drive that would be taking place on the following Friday.

SPCA Log Notes

(Just as I was about to start logging I got a very loose
idea for the Anchor Intro and wrote it down.)

THE SPCA TYPICALLY TAKES IN AND ADOPTS OUT 5,000 ANIMALS
A YEAR. BUT THIS PAST YEAR THEY'VE HAD MORE ANIMALS BEING
BROUGHT IN — RELINQUICHED BY OWNERS WHO, BECAUSE OF THE
ECONOMY, CAN NO LONGER AFFORD TO KEEP THEIR PETS — AND
THE NUMBER OF PEOPLE ADOPTING PETS IS DOWN. A TEN PERCENT
INCREASE IN JUST ONE YEAR. SOMETHING THE SPCA HASN'T SEEN
BEFORE.

RICK JOHNSON, SACRAMENTO SPCA
Cl 58   .40
Forrest is a 4 yr old Lab who was relinquished by a
family.

1.09
I would anticipate he'll find a home pretty darn quick.

(As I transcribed this bite, I came up with a line of
track and wrote it into the log.)

FORREST MAY BECOME OF THE LUCKY ONES, BUT HE IS ONE OF
THE **UNLUCKY** 500 CATS, DOGS, BIRDS, RABBITS AND OTHER
ANIMALS THAT ARE **UNLUCKY** ENOUGH TO BE CALLING THE
SACRAMENTO S.P.C.A. HOME.

1.39
Unfortunately with Forrest, he was given up. But he will
find a home. 1.48
1.58

We're seeing this year a huge number of animals
relinquished by families.

2.20
..they don't have money to pay vet bills or even feed the
animals. 2.26

2.38
We're also seeing a reduction in the number of adoptions.

Cl 60   3.50
Sit. That's a good boy.

4.15
Sit. Yeah-good boy-good boy.

Cl 61   4.38
Our rabbits will be $1.11. 4.41

Cl 65   5.37
All of these animals were relinquished by owners for a
multitude of reasons. 4.44

Cl 72   7.50
We come in in the morning and there're boxes of cats or
there are dogs put in our fenced area. 7.56

ON A NORMAL DAY THE SPCA IS LUCKY TO ADOPT OUT 70-80
ANIMALS. BU ON FRIDAY, NOVEMBER 11 — 11-11 —

8.27
We're looking to place 111 animals in new homes in one
day.

THAT'S RIGHT — 111 ANIMALS. THAT'S DOGS, CATS, EVEN BIRDS
AND RABBITS.

Cl 73   8.45
That would be a record for us to achieve that, but we
think we can do it.

9.24
We're going to open from 11.11 in the morning to 11.11 at
night.

Cl 92   19.05
Sasha came to us because of a foreclosure.

JOAN THOMPSON, SPCA Volunteer
Cl 102   24.20
They're so happy to get outside.

Cl 103   25.33
People have lost their homes, they're going into
apartments, can't keep their pets, simply can't afford
them.

25.50
Because of the circumstance—because of the economy—people
can't keep them. It's very sad.

26.09
How do you give something like this up?

26.50
Most of them, they just want—they just want somebody to
love them.

Writing The Script – First Draft

Once the footage is logged I know what I have to work with. I make a copy of that document in Word, then go through and cut out all the bites that are weak, rambling or vague. Since the package can only run 1:15-1:20, I only focus on the best sound that I have.

As I've mentioned, I don't want my voice to be the dominant voice that the viewers hear. I want the people in the story to tell the story as much as possible. So I begin moving bites around in a way that tells a story—opening with a bite, followed by more bites that convey information, and an interesting, amusing or emotional bit of sound with which to wrap the package up at the end.

Once I've gone through the bites I'll look at whatever tracks I've already written to determine whether they can work or not.

Then it's time to actually write some lines of track to connect everything together from start to finish. For this, I keep a few things in mind:

- Keep the sentences short. Just a sentence or two per track.
- Fill sentences with facts and information that will be new to the folks watching at home. There are only 75 seconds to tell this story. No unnecessary words.
- Keep the writing conversational so that it can be spoken easily.

This is my first draft script:

```
ANCHOR INTRO
[I know this is long. Perhaps to have the lines alternate
between the two anchors with rolling video in the
background?]

THE SACRAMENTO SPCA TYPICALLY TAKES IN AND ADOPTS OUT
5,000 ANIMALS A YEAR, BUT THIS PAST YEAR THEY'VE HAD MORE
ANIMALS BEING BROUGHT IN. IT'S ANOTHER SAD SIGN OF OUR
ECONOMIC TIMES — OWNERS WHO'VE LOST THEIR HOMES AND CAN
NO LONGER AFFORD TO KEEP OR EVEN FEED THEIR PETS. AND THE
NUMBER OF PEOPLE ADOPTING PETS IS ALSO DOWN. KCRA 3'S
MIKE CARROLL SHOWS US HOW TOMORROW THE SPCA IS DOING A
VERY SPECIAL ONE-DAY EVENT TO HELP GET SOME OF THESE PETS
INTO NEW HOMES— AND WHERE YOU CAN HELP — AND SAVE A LOT
OF MONEY AT THE SAME TIME.

RICK JOHNSON, SACRAMENTO SPCA
Cl 58  .40
Forrest is a 4 yr old Lab who was relinquished by a
family.

1.09
I would anticipate he'll find a home pretty darn quick.
```

FORREST MAY BECOME OF THE LUCKY ONES, BUT HE IS ONE OF
THE **UNLUCKY** 400 CATS, DOGS, BIRDS, RABBITS AND OTHER
ANIMALS THAT ARE **UNLUCKY** ENOUGH TO CURRENTLY BE CALLING
THE SACRAMENTO S.P.C.A. HOME.

ON AN AVERAGE DAY ABOUT 25 TO 30 PETS COMING INTO THE
SPCA.

Cl 72   7.50
We come in in the morning and there're boxes of cats or
there are dogs put in our fenced area. 7.56

CL 58   2.20
..they don't have money to pay vet bills or even feed the
animals. 2.26

AND BEING ADOPTED OUT EVERY DAY.

1.58
We're seeing this year a huge number of animals
relinquished by families. 2.02

SO THE SPCA IS TAKING ACTION. THIS FRIDAY, NOVEMBER 11 —
11-11 — THEY WANT TO GET 111 PETS INTO NEW HOMES — IN ONE
DAY.

CL 73   9.24
We're going to open from 11.11 in the morning to 11.11 at
night.

TO ACHIEVE THIS THEY'RE SLASHING THEIR ADOPTION FEES. IT
NORMALLY COSTS ABOUT A HUNDRED DOLLARS TO ADOPT A DOG. ON
11-11 YOU CAN TAKE HOME A DOG OR CAT FOR JUST $11.11.

THEY EVEN HAVE BIRDS AND RABBITS.

Cl 61   4.38
Our rabbits will be $1.11. 4.41

IN SACRAMENTO, I'M MIKE CARROLL, KCRA-3 REPORTS.

ANCHOR TAG:

THE SPCA ADDS DURING THEIR ONE-DAY ADOPT-A-THON THAT IN
ADDITION TO THAT ELEVEN DOLLARS AND ELEVEN CENTS, YOU
ALSO GET TWO WEEKS OF PET FOOD FREE.

Final Broadcast Script

The importance of the first draft is to stitch the whole story together from beginning to end, giving me an idea of how long it runs. In this case, 1:35 to 1:45. The next step is to finesse the script, reworking sentences or writing new ones to make it clearer, as well as condensing or deleting tracks and bites.

This is the draft I submitted to the E.P.

```
INTRO
TOMORROW IS 11-11-11 AND IN HONOR OF
THE DATE AND IN HONOR OF THE DATE
THE SACRAMENTO SPCA HAS A SPECIAL
OFFER IF YOU'RE THINKING OF ADOPTING
A PET. AS KCRA'S MIKE CARROLL
REPORTS TONIGHT, IT'S AN OPPORTUNITY
TO GET A NEW FRIEND AND SAVE A LOT
OF MONEY AT THE SAME TIME.
```

```
RICK JOHNSON, SACRAMENTO SPCA
Forrest is a 4 year old Lab who was
relinquished by a family.
```

```
FORREST WAS ONE OF THE 25 TO 30 PETS
WHO COME INTO THE SACRAMENTO
S.P.C.A. EVERY DAY.
```

```
RICK JOHNSON, SACRAMENTO SPCA
We come in in the morning and
there're boxes of cats or there are
dogs put in our fenced area. 7.56
```

```
ECONOMIC TIMES THAT ARE MAKING
FAMILY PETS HOMELESS AS WELL.
```

```
RICK JOHNSON, SACRAMENTO SPCA
Sasha came to us because of a
foreclosure.
```

THIS IS SOMETHING THE SPCA HAS NEVER
SEEN BEFORE.

JOAN THOMPSON, SPCA VOLUNTEER
Because of the economy, people just
can't keep them. And it's very sad.

SO THEY'RE TAKING ACTION. THIS
FRIDAY, NOVEMBER 11 — 11-11 — THEY
WANT TO GET 111 PETS INTO NEW HOMES
— IN ONE DAY.

RICK JOHNSON, SACRAMENTO SPCA
We're going to open from 11:11 in
the morning to 11:11 at night.

TO ACHIEVE THIS THEY'RE SLASHING
THEIR ADOPTION FEES. IT NORMALLY
COSTS ABOUT A HUNDRED DOLLARS TO
ADOPT A DOG. ON 11-11 YOU CAN TAKE
HOME A DOG OR CAT FOR JUST $11.11.

JOAN THOMPSON, SPCA VOLUNTEER
They're so happy to be outside.

JOAN THOMPSON VOLUNTEERS AT THE
SPCA, TAKING THE DOGS OUT FOR WALKS.

JOAN THOMPSON, SPCA VOLUNTEER
How do you give something like this
up?

A ONE DAY, TWELVE HOUR EVENT THAT
COULD CHANGE THE LIFE OF A PET LIKE
THIS.

JOAN THOMPSON, SPCA VOLUNTEER
They just want somebody to love
them.

IN SACRAMENTO, I'M MIKE CARROLL,
KCRA-3 REPORTS.

ANCHOR TAG:

THE SPCA ADDS DURING THEIR ONE-DAY
ADOPT-A-THON THAT IN ADDITION TO
THAT ELEVEN DOLLARS AND ELEVEN
CENTS, YOU ALSO GET TWO WEEKS OF PET
FOOD FREE.

As a follow-up, on November 11, 2011, the day of the Adopt-A-Thon, lines started forming outside the Sacramento SPCA at eight in the morning. There was such a public response that people were having to park up to a quarter mile away. The SPCA wound up opening their doors early. By mid-afternoon all 400 pets had been adopted and pets were brought in from other Sacramento animal shelters to help fill the need. In all, over 600 pets were adopted into new homes on that day.

QUICK TURNAROUND: Land Park Volunteer Corps

One of the advantages to working in this business is that if there is a subject or organization that you know and care about, you can get the chance to do a story about it and help to spread the word about what they are doing.

Near where I live in Sacramento is William S. Land Park, or simply Land Park for short, which is truly one of the city's gems. Created in the 1920s, the park has been maintained for the past ninety years by a professional staff of City of Sacramento workers. However, due to the nation-wide financial crisis, the city has had to impose severe budget cuts that have led to the park staff being reduced to a mere handful, not a sufficient amount to keep the park up to the standards that the public expects. A friend helped to organize the Land Park Volunteer Corps, a group of a hundred residents from the surrounding neighborhoods who pitch in a few hours on the first Saturday of each month to trim trees, plant flowerbeds and pull weeds. When he told me about this effort I said this would be a great story to let people know what some of its residents were doing.

I pitched the story to the assignment desk on a Friday and got approved to shoot the clean up on Saturday morning. Ideally, I wanted to spend forty-five minutes to an hour profiling a couple of the volunteers at work, as well as talk to a few people enjoying the park and get their reaction as to how the place was looking.

However, when I came into work that Saturday morning I was told that there'd been a rash of overnight shootings in Stockton, about forty miles south of Sacramento, which the producers wanted for their lead story. I was needed to load into a live truck and head there with KCRA reporter Sharokina Shams (who was given her start in television by news director Julie Akins, interviewed earlier in this book). But the producers still wanted to run a 30-second VO-SOT on the Land Park clean up and for us to take ten or fifteen minutes to swing by on our way out of town, grab a quick VO or VO-SOT and feed it back from Stockton for a producer to write up and an editor to cut for the five o'clock news.

It's so common in TV news for the best laid plans to have to be put aside to make way for breaking news. It just goes with the job. But I still wanted to try and do more than just a VO-SOT, yet still shoot it in the fifteen minutes that I was being given.

I hadn't turned a reporter package in several weeks and wanted to get back into the system. (I'm vain—I like hearing my name on TV.) I decided to make this a challenge to see how quickly I could shoot and gather all the interviews, as well as write and edit the package—in addition to shooting, editing and running the live truck for our other lead story.

We pulled up at Land Park where a group with the Land Park Volunteer Corps was working. Sharokina had her laptop open, researching the overnight police reports for the Stockton story.

"Keep working on your story," I said to her. "I'll grab this. Be back in fifteen minutes."

I grabbed the camera and a stick mic and, determined to make use of every second of the fifteen minutes that I had, was rolling on the workers as I walked up to them. I talked to three or four people, asking only a few quick questions of each. "Tell me what's going on here?" "Why do you want to be here doing this on a Saturday morning?" "About all this work you're doing, do you think it's making a difference?" In the responses, everyone addressed the budget cutbacks and layoffs. One woman even made a specific comment that another city maintenance worker had been laid off only a few days before. I knew that would be a bite that I'd have to write to.

The B-roll was grabbed just as quickly in between the interviews, shooting in my "active camera" style of shooting long shot, medium shot and close-up all in the same walking handheld shot. When I packed the camera and mic back into the truck and fired up to continue on south to Stockton there were barely nine minutes of footage to work with.

I called back to the station and told the producer that I could turn it into a quick package. I also let him know that I didn't have a laptop with me so I wouldn't be able to write it up formally and e-mail it back for his approval, that I'd just have to crank it out and feed it back. If he didn't like the package then I'd feed back the raw footage and he could run it just as a regular VO-SOT. "I'm sure that whatever you send me will be fine," he replied. "Call me after it's fed and you can tell me what the intro, tag and fonts are."

On the drive down to Stockton I scribbled down some tracks on the back of some script pages that had been left in the truck. Hardly one of the cleanest scripts I've ever written.

The only bite that I definitely knew I wanted to write to was the one about the recently laid off maintenance worker. The rest of the tracks were written in a general style, summing up the situation of the poor economy, city budget woes, park employee cutbacks and layoffs, and the people around Land Park rallying to keep the park alive and beautiful.

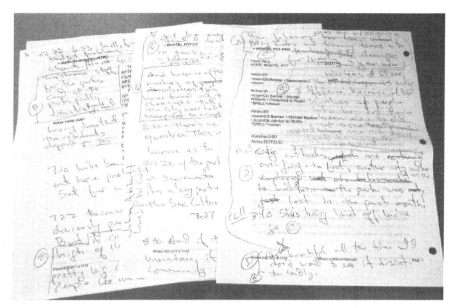

When we got to Stockton, Sharokina and I grabbed a quick lunch break before we were scheduled to meet up with a spokesperson from the Stockton Police Department to interview for our main story. I munched in the live truck as I quickly logged the couple of short interviews I had. Since I'd kept my interviews short it was much faster to select the bites. In fact, my notes had been scribbled down in such a jumble that I had to number the paragraphs as "1," "2," "3," and annotate the interview bites as "A," "B," "C," in order to keep track of what went where.

From there, Sharokina and I went to the Stockton Police Department to interview their spokesperson, then drove to the neighborhood where the shootings took place. Later in the afternoon, while Sharokina was writing her five o'clock script, I recorded my audio track and laid down the A-roll. By that time, Sharokina was ready with her track. I started editing our primary story at four o'clock. By 4:20 our lead story was finished and I switched over to filling in the Land Park story with B-roll. By 4:27 that story was finished as well—speed-cutting to see how tight a deadline I could work under. By 4:30 I was feeding both stories back to the station.

In the end, this was a bonus story for the station. The producers, who had only hoped for a 30-second reader, were handed a fully-written, tracked and edited package, and the Land Park Volunteer Corps got some on-air coverage. So a win-win all around.

SCRIPT: Land Park Volunteer Corps

INTRO:
SACRAMENTO IS KNOWN AS "THE CITY
OF TREES" AND YOU COULD CERTAINLY
TELL THAT IN THE CITY PARKS. BUT
RECENT BUDGET CUTS HAVE LEFT SOME
PART SUFFERING. KCRA 3'S MIKE
CARROLL SHOWS US NOW HOW
BEIGHBORS AROUND WILLIAM LAND
PARK ARE RALLYING TO KEEP THEIR
PARK GREEN.

TAKE PKG:

SOT:
Well, the park is really a
treasure in this part of town. It
really is.

WILLIAM LAND PARK IS IN CONSTANT
USE BY PICNICKERS, GOLFERS AND
SPORTS TEAMS, TO NAME A FEW.
UNFORTUNATELY, THE CITY CAN NO
LONGER AFFORD TO KEEP IT
CONSTANTLY MAINTAINED.

JOHN ABBOT, LAND PARK VOLUNTEER
CORPS
The budget problems, everybody
knows about. They had to cut back
the maintenance staff in the parks
-- in all the parks in the city
pretty dramatically.

AND CITY CUTBACKS ARE ON-GOING. IN
FACT, ANOTHER CITY WORKER AT THE
PARK WAS LET GO IN JUST THE PAST
MONTH.

NAN JOHNSON, LAND PARK VOLUNTEER
CORPS
She's being laid off. We're going
to miss her.

NAN JOHNSON JOINED THE LAND PARK
VOLUNTEER CORPS NEARLY A YEAR AGO,
TRIMMING TREES AND PULLING WEEDS.

NAN JOHNSON, LAND PARK VOLUNTEER
CORPS
It's a way of repaying the
community.

JOHN ABBOT, LAND PARK VOLUNTEER
CORPS
It draws anywhere from 50 to maybe
a high of 110. We draw a pretty
big crowd. I mean, there's a lot
of people who are concerned about
this park.

THE VOLUNTEERS AT LAND PARK ARE
MAKING A DIFFERENCE. BECAUSE OF
THE NUMBERS OF PEOPLE WHO TURN
OUT, THEY'VE BEEN ABLE TO CLEAN
UP AREAS THAT THE CITY NEVER HAD
THE MANPOWER TO MAINTAIN.

JOHN ABBOT, LAND PARK VOLUNTEER
CORPS
We found a stone wall that I don't
think anybody's seen in years.

LOUISE DRIGGS, LAND PARK VOLUNTEER
CORPS
And it's a beautiful day to be
outside, that's a plus. If it'd
been raining, I don't know.

AT WILLIAM LAND PARK IN
SACRAMENTO, I'M MIKE CARROLL FOR
KCRA-3 REPORTS.

TAG:
VOLUNTEERS USUALLY SHOW UP AT 8:30
ON THE FIRST SATURDAY OF EACH
MONTH TO PITCH IN.

EDITING

Ashleigh Walters edits her story using Final Cut in a microwave truck in the field.

The two keys to editing TV news:

Only use the best of what you've shot.

Cut it as fast as you can.

YOU'RE NEW AT THE JOB AND JUST STARTING OUT. The deadline clock is ticking and you've got to start editing, which could be on the very same laptop that you just finished writing your story on. Panic is setting in. "Oh my gosh, I've got all this stuff and no time to get it done. I've only got a minute and ten seconds to get *all* of this stuff in, plus my bites *and* my stand-up. How am I going to get those in?"

The short answer is: You don't.

The Bottom Line in Editing: **Only use your *best* material.**

The biggest mistake you can make is to try to jam too much into your story. Don't even try it. Too many people try to put in as many shots as they can, making each one very short and quick, in the end looking like a series of flash cards. That's too fast and disorienting for the viewers. You're not going to have enough time to sort through your footage to make all those cuts in the first place.

KCRA chief photographer (and frequent reporter-photographer) Mike Rhinehart edits a story with reporter David Bienick in the field in a satellite truck.

Whenever you have doubts about what to do, one phrase will get you through every time: **"Keep it simple, stupid."**

If you've got a line of track that runs ten seconds and you've got six shots that show what you're describing—only use the one shot that illustrates that sentence best. Just because you've got a lot of shots doesn't mean you have to use them all.

As I've described earlier, I shoot almost everything in an "active camera" style where the camera is always moving, either handheld or panning and zooming, so my footage has lots of movement in it. A locked down, static shot that doesn't have movement is only interesting for 3 to 5 seconds. Then you need to cut to something else. But an "active camera" shot with movement in it can hold the viewer's attention for 10 seconds easily, or even 20 or 30 seconds if the activity is interesting.

Another phrase that I keep in mind when cutting a package on a crazy deadline is, **"You only have to fill a minute and ten seconds."** I'm not editing a documentary or a five-minute magazine segment—I only have to fill 1:10 of news. My whole eight-hour day may be just about filling 70 seconds of "air time." If I delete the two or three bites and the stand-up, that leaves me with only 25 to 30 seconds to cover with B-roll. If the story's shot in locked-down static shots with a new cut every two or three or four seconds, that's about a dozen shots. If it's shot in "active camera" style, that's only five or six shots.

KCRA reporter Sharokina Shams records her track in an audio booth.

Recording Reporter Audio Track

The first step after having a script approved is to record an audio track—also known as "cutting audio" or "cutting a track."

When editing at the station the standard practice is to cut your track in an audio booth, which is typically in the editing area. In the field you can record the track into a laptop using an audio program, though most often people just record their audio straight into the camera.

Many people assume that recording a track is simple—just read your script into a microphone. Actually it's a skill that only comes from doing it over and over and "finding your voice"—the pace and level that works best for you.

Cutting a track is much more than just reading a script out loud. The goal is to sound like you're telling a story off the top of your head and not reading anything at all.

There are several schools of thought on the best way to do this. A voice coach once

In a live truck in the field, KCRA reporter Mallory Hoff records her track from a script written on her Blackberry.

encouraged me to just relax and say it casually, naturally, almost conversationally.

Another approach is to be very fast and high-energy to squeeze a lot of information into a 1:15-1:20 package. Personally, I can't talk that fast without getting tongue-tied. So I go for a third option.

I strive to keep my scripts tight, giving weight to each word. So I use a strong delivery, putting emphasis on key words to drive the information home to the viewer. Every time I go into the audio booth I still hear my first news director Steve Ramsey saying, "You can't over-exaggerate your voice too much."

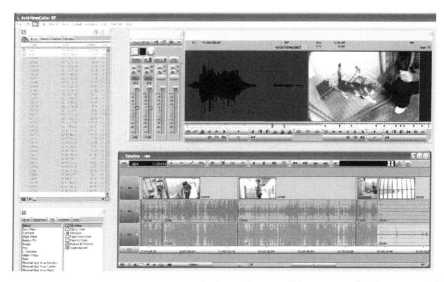

The Avid Newscutter screen, a typical non-linear editing setup. On the upper left is the **Bin** where all the clips are loaded. Next over is the **Audio Mixer** for adjusting sound levels. In the center is the **Source Window** where a clip from the Bin is opened and In and Out Points are set for "dropping" clips onto the timeline. A reporter audio track is in the Source Window, as displayed by the waveform symbol. On the upper left is the **Timeline Window**, where the edited footage on the timeline is displayed. Across the bottom of the screen runs the **Timeline**, where the editing is done. This Timeline is displaying raw footage clips in chronological order to give me an idea of the material I have to work with. All of these various elements of the screen are scalable and can be made larger or smaller to your own personal preferences. **NOTE:** The setup displayed above is the same way that I always work, whether it's in Avid Newscutter, Adobe Premier or Final Cut Pro, the non-linear editing programs I've worked with.

Editing Terminology

Every technical process has a language of its own. If you have any experience with simple home computer editing, such as iMovie, the terminology and the process are similar. If you have editing software on your computer it would be wise to become familiar with it.

All discussion here will be with regards to non-linear editing on a computer. There may still be some small-market, hold-out stations that are still shooting on tape and editing machine-to-machine, but those days are numbered. For one thing, parts for those systems haven't been made in years, so it's only a matter of time.

- When shooting a story you're gathering **shots**.
- In editing, shots are now referred to as **clips**.
- Clips are **imported** or **loaded** into the computer.

- In the computer, clips are filed into a **folder**, a **bin** or a **browser**—the name varies depending on the editing program you're working in.
- The editing is done on a **timeline**.
- To move a clip from a bin onto the timeline is to **drag** it.
- Cutting clips on the timeline may require a **blade** tool.
- To send a finished, edited story out of the computer is to **send**, **export** or **upload** it.

Most stations are tapeless as of this writing in February 2012, meaning that the edited story is **sent** directly from the computer into a station **server**. From there it's retrieved by a technician in the control room for playback on the news.

Some stations which don't have a server will **export** or **burn** stories to a tape or disk. A technician will then load the tape or disk into a playback deck and roll each story manually during the newscast.

Edit As You Go

In this method, you edit your A-roll and your B-roll in sequential order, building the package as you go.

- Lay down the opening snippet of natural sound.
- Lay down the first reporter audio track.
- Cover the first reporter track with B-roll.
- Put in the first bite, or couple of bites.
- Lay down the next reporter track.
- Cover that track with B-roll up to the next interview bite, and so on.

The argument for this method is that if you're running out of time to edit, you can feed back or upload your package as it is up to that point, albeit uncompleted, then explain the rest of the story as a live reporter tag. It's one way of at least getting the story on the air.

The danger to working this way is that you run the risk of spending more time laying down the A-roll track and bites and covering the package as you go, only to find out in the end that the package is too long and you have to start cutting out bits to get it "down to time." That's a lot of time wasted editing parts of a story that are never going to be used.

KCRA intern Nha Nguyen learns to edit on the Avid Newscutter.

Challenge Yourself With False Deadlines

When I started out I'd hear reporters saying about new shooters, "He's such a nice guy."

"Yeah—and he's so fast."

If you can be both good at what you do *and* fast at doing it, then your value in the workplace goes way up.

When you start out in this business you're given a fair amount of leeway because you need to learn the gear, the editing system, the station computer system and so on. You're typically given about an hour to edit a package, but you're not always going to have an hour. There could be computer issues that will push you back. There could also be a last minute update to the story, requiring the entire package to be reworked.

When I'm learning something new, I give myself time to become familiar with it. But after that I start ramping it up by creating **false deadlines** to force myself to work faster. I'll start cutting my hour edit time down to 45 minutes, then 30 minutes, until I'm down to 25 minutes or less.

I don't focus on becoming expert at all the ins and outs of the editing system—only what I need to know to cut a package. I can learn more of the special features over time. My daily job is doing daily news so my emphasis is on what I need to know to get through the day—and *fast*.

> **Bottom Line:** When editing news, faster is better. Look for editing shortcuts. Strive to be the fastest cutter in your shop.

My Editing Method

I don't know any two editors who edit the same way—and every editor thinks their way is the best. The bottom line is that everyone has to figure out what works best for them. Every reporter I work with tells me that I'm one of the fastest editors they know, so I'm going to describe step-by-step how I edit a package.

To illustrate this, I'm using the footage from the SPCA Adopt-A-Thon, which was detailed earlier in the section on writing.

Visual Preferences—The Non-Visual Timeline

Non linear editing is a visual editing system. Video is represented on the timeline as a collared rectangle and the accompanying audio is represented as differently colored rectangles. However, when I see editors work on timelines where the video and audio rectangles are completely blank (and *non*-visual) I don't see how they can edit. "How do you know which shot is which? And how can you see the audio to know where to make your cuts? How can you find anything?"

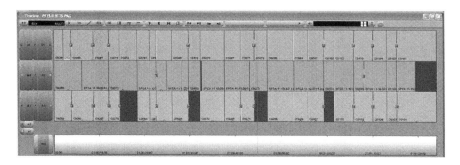

Visual Preferences—The Visual Timeline—"I Want To See Everything!"

I want to *see* my shots *and* the audio.

In **Timeline Preferences** (which is in different places in Avid, Final Cut Pro, Adobe Premiere and the other editing programs out there) select **Clip Frames**, which displays the first frame of video of each clip on the timeline. This immediately identifies the clip as an interview bite, establishing shot, close-up, etc.

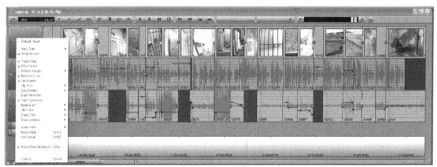

The white pop-up panel, seen above on the left, is for the **Timeline Preferences**. Here, in Avid Newscutter, you can select **Clip Frames** to see the first frame of every shot and **Audio Settings** to display **waveforms**.

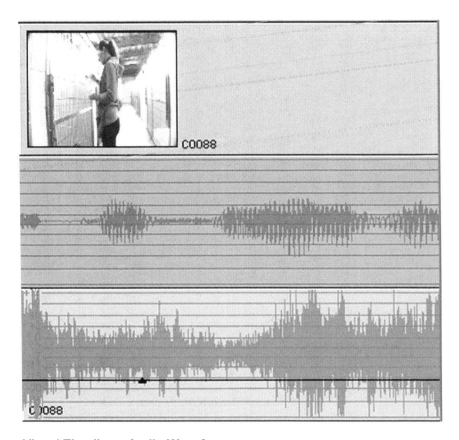

Visual Timeline—Audio Waveforms

I also use the **Preferences** to display the **Audio Waveforms** of the clips. This is a visual display of the sound of a clip, which looks something like a Richter scale graph. For instance, a door slam or a baseball bat connecting with a ball will appear as a sharp spike. This permits you to see where in the clip the audio is occurring. It's especially helpful when cutting interview bites to be able to see when a person starts and stops speaking.

Raw Footage Timeline

Once I have all my story clips and the clip with my reporter audio track loaded into the bin, my next step is to create two timelines. One is for all my raw footage and the other is the timeline for editing the package.

I drag every clip of raw footage I have to work with down onto the **raw footage timeline** in sequential order. When I need a shot I can click on this timeline and rapidly scroll across it to find either a specific shot I'm looking for or simply a shot that can work.

Since I shoot with an "active camera," the first frame on a clip won't display everything that's on that clip. By scrolling the cursor across the timeline I can see (in the viewer window on the upper left) the action in the clips to quickly find a clip with the type of action that I need. This is much faster than clicking through clips individually in the bin.

Make Notes Of The B-Roll To Work With

Just before I start laying down the B-roll, I'll scroll through the timeline and select shots to "drop into the timeline," either as a series of shots or as a single continuous shot, and will jot down the clip numbers in the margin of the script alongside the paragraph of reporter track where the shots can work.

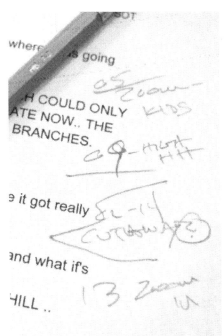

Having a list of the shots and where to use them will save time from having to constantly alternate back and forth between the edit timeline and the raw timeline searching for "cover" shots.

Time is precious on a deadline. Any shortcut that can speed the process is valuable.

Laying Down The A-Roll—1) The Reporter Track

Time to get cutting.

First, I "lay down the **A-roll**." The A-roll is the primary audio and video in a package—the reporter audio track, interview bites and any specific bits of natural sound that have been directly written to.

I drag my **reporter audio clip** down onto the **edit timeline** onto **Audio Channel One**. I place it about 1½ to 2 seconds in from the beginning of the timeline to allow for a "nat sot pop off the top"—a quick snippet of natural sound to start the piece. This also helps to separate the anchor's voice, who just intro'd the story from my voice track.

My reporter track audio is one complete clip containing all the four to six or so tracks in the script. Each track is a new paragraph in the script and are typically recorded as, "Track one, take one. Five—four—three—two—one." Then the audio track of that scripted paragraph begins. Each separate track will be punctuated by interview bites or natural sound on the timeline.

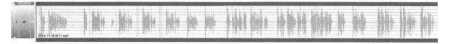

By editing audio in waveforms it's easy to see the separation between the different tracks. It's also easy to spot my "false starts"—where I flubbed my speech and started over, or felt that I wasn't strong enough on the first take—because, since I'm saying exactly the same words, the waveform patterns for that second or third take of a line will look identical because I'm saying exactly the same words. The waveforms allow me to *see* my audio so I hardly have to even listen to it. I cut out all the countdowns ("Five—four—three—"), flubs and mistakes so that the reporter track of the edit is clean from start to finish. In less than a minute I'll have the reporter track "laid down."

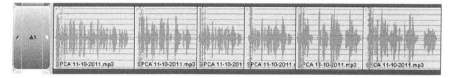

Laying Down The A-Roll—2) Adding The Bites

The next step is to **insert** the **bites** and specific natural sound onto the timeline using the **Video Track** and **Audio Channel One** to complete the **A-roll**. Since the clip numbers and timecodes for the bites are written down in the script, this only takes a few minutes.

For example, one of the clips in the SPCA script is for "Clip 72 7:50-7:56." I click on the Clip 72 to bring it into the viewer. On the **Viewer Timeline**, I set an **In-Point** at 7:52 and **Out-Point** at 7:56, then **insert** that bite in between my first and second reporter tracks on the **editing timeline**.

Clip 72
The counter here on the upper corner indicates the **timecode** of the clip. It's currently 7:57, the end of the bite to be used.

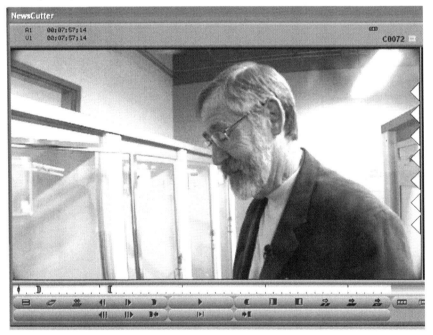

The two tiny tabs, like brackets, on the white line are the **In Point** and the **Out Point** for the bite to be inserted to the timeline.

There's usually a bit of excess "slop" at the front and the back—the "top" and the "tail"—of a bite when it's brought onto the timeline. With audio waveforms it's easy to see where the bite begins and ends, so trimming the front and the back of the clip to make the bite precise is done in seconds.

I do the same thing with all the rest of the bites and pieces of natural sound to complete the A-roll. This takes 3 to 5 minutes.

I edit these clips tightly so that by the time the A-roll is finished I can see what the **TRT** (total running time) of the story is. If the TRT is 1:20 (one minute and twenty seconds), then I'm fine.

On the other hand, if the TRT's 1:25 or 1:30 or more, then I have to cut out a line of track or tighten up a bite or two. If there's a bite where someone uses two sentences to say something, I may have to chop it down to one sentence to get it down to a "final run time" of 1:20 or 1:15.

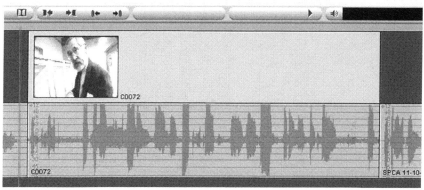

BEFORE:
Notice how there is a little extra audio "slop" on either end of the bite.

AFTER:
The bite after it's been tightened. It will now be much cleaner flowing out of the reporter audio track. The edits are slight, but make a big difference when played back.

The highlighted area in the middle of the timeline is the first part of the interview bite with SPCA volunteer Joan Thompson, seen just to the right panel of the highlighted area. There was a pause of a few seconds when Joan was speaking, which I cut out, then brought the front and the back audio cuts of her bite together. I then extended the B-roll shot of another volunteer caring for dogs inside the kennels over the first audio clip of Joan's bite and up to the last part of her bite, which was seen on-camera. The diagonal slashes seen on the Video Track and on Audio Channel Two are Dissolves.

"Minor Surgery"—Tightening Up A Bite

It's not uncommon to have a bite where the person will take a while to say something, such as, "Well, I was never for certain. . . . uh. . . . just how this deal was gonna work. But. . . . uh. . . . I guess. . . . uh. . . . in the end. . . . uh. . . . it all worked out."

A bite like that could easily run 15 to 20 very long seconds—or almost one-fifth of the total time you have for the whole package. Yet, it might be just the bite you need. In that case, it's a bite that needs some trimming.

Whenever I have a bite with a long pause or someone saying "uh" once too often, I cut them out. "Chop out the dead air."

To hide the edit, I'll then cover that portion of the bite with B-roll, usually by extending the B-roll shot that either led into the bite or that's following after the bite.

The 15 or 20 second bite will now be, "Well, I was never for certain [Cut] just how this deal was gonna work. But [Cut] in the end [Cut] it all worked out."

It could even be trimmed down more to, "Well, I was never for certain [Cut] just how this deal was gonna work. But [Cut] it all worked out."

You haven't changed any of the meaning of what was said and the person will thank you for making them sound better. You will also have kept your story moving, instead of bringing it to a virtual dead stop. And you won't have to suffer the ire of a producer demanding to know why your package came in at a jaw-dropping 1:30 instead of the 1:15 that you were given.

Laying Down The B-Roll—3) "Covering The Black"

Once I get to this stage I feel like I'm on a downhill run speeding to the finish line.

The interview bites typically make up between 25-40 seconds of the 1:10-1:20 package. The job now is to edit **B-roll** over the 40-50 seconds of reporter track to "fill in the holes," "cover the black" or "make the black go away." I'm not covering over the whole story, only the reporter track portions of the timeline between the bites.

This is where **the story is visually told** so that the folks at home can see what the story is about. The goal here is to use the best shots that I have out of the 10 to 20 minutes of B-roll I've shot, matching the video to what's being said. I try to edit shots to cut with the rhythm and punctuation of the audio track. At a comma, make a cut, end of a sentence, another cut. I'll sacrifice a really good shot that's not moving in favor of another shot that has movement in order to maintain a visual momentum that will drive the story to the end.

Laying in the B-roll can take 10 to 25 minutes. (In a crunch it can be done in 5 minutes or less, which I will describe later.)

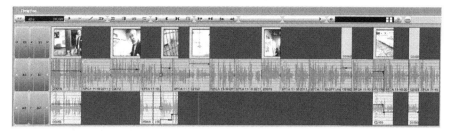

At the end of the opening bite or bit of natural sound I'll set an **In-Point** on the **video timeline** and on **Audio Channel 2**, which I am using for background natural sound. (Remember, **Audio Channel 1** has the reporter track and interview bites.) This audio will play at a significantly lower level, anywhere from 50% to 20% of full volume, so as not to interfere with the reporter track. I'll then set an **Out-Point** at the very beginning of the next sound bite. Over this space of 5 to 20 seconds of reporter track, which is at present "black hole," I must cover with B-roll.

There are no absolute hard-and-fast rules on how B-roll is supposed to be used. There are always the basics to fall back on—open with a wide establishing shot, then work your way in with medium shots and close-ups. But if you don't want to open with an establishing shot of a dentist's office, thinking it's more dramatic to start with a big close-up of a dentist's drill completely filling the frame, then go for it.

Try a series of many shots edited very fast together, or just use a few shots that you decide to hold on so that the viewers at home can see the detail of what they are looking at. Cut the story any way you want. Editing, just like photography and writing, is subjective. There are myriads of ways to use and arrange shots.

A producer is never going to say to you, "Nice package. But that medium shot that was the third shot in should have come after the establishing shot." Producers only want the story to look good, not have any "black holes," be in on time, and be under 1:20.

Once I've covered the first hole, I'll move on to cover the next piece of reporter track, set my In and Out Points, cover that section, and continue on until the package is filled in. Then I'll push the story to the server, from which it will be played on air.

In local news, the finished story is almost never reviewed by anyone except you, the reporter-photographer. Producers have their hands full with writing and putting their newscasts together. People outside of the news business are always amazed when I tell them this, but this is how it's worked at every station I've worked at. Producers will review the script, but almost never see the finished story until it goes on the air.

The only hard-and-fast rules in editing are:

- "Don't leave any black"—cover every single frame with video.
- Finish the story and upload it so that it "makes air."

Bottom Line: If you don't meet the deadline and your story doesn't make air, then it won't be the story that matters, it will be whether you still have a job in this business or not. A hard general rule about TV and deadlines is that it's a lot like baseball—three strikes and you're out.

The highlighted area between the In and Out Points set to "fill the hole," in this case about 12 seconds.

Speed-Editing—Long-Running Shots To Fill The Holes

When I'm really up against a deadline I will simply set an In-point at the end of one interview bite, then an Out-point at the beginning of the next interview bite. This "hole" may run anywhere from 4 to 15 seconds. Then I'll simply grab the best looking bit of active video that I have in one continuous shot and drop that in to cover the whole space.

If need be, I'll do this to fill all the "black" in the whole story. Find a shot with a nice slow zoom that will work for 5 to 11 seconds—lay it in. Find a handheld shot with good movement and action—in it goes.

The bottom line in TV news is to "get it on the air." If you can do it fast *and* make it pretty, all the better.

One single long-running shot with visual action, where the camera is either physically moving with the action or panning and zooming with action to keep the viewer's eye stimulated.

Rough Edits—Make Them Pretty With Dissolves

If the video works for the track, but is a little visually jarring in the beginning or ending edit points, I'll throw in a 10 to 20 frame **Dissolve**. A simple fix that *always* makes a transition from one shot to another look prettier.

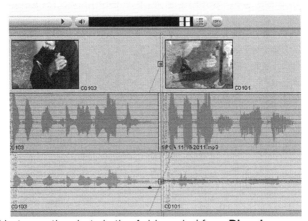

The "slash" between the shots is the Avid symbol for a **Dissolve**.

Notice that the dissolve is on both the video channel and audio channel 2. A dissolve will not only blend from one shot to the next, but will also blend the audio, making the natural sound transition smoother. (Audio channel 1, seen here in the middle, is for reporter track and interview bites and remains untouched.

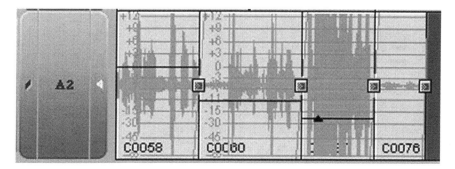

Smoothing The Audio With Dissolves

Most of the stories I work on visually are straight-cuts from shot to shot. However, I'll use lots of quick **transitions** on the **audio timeline**, either Channel 1 or Channel 2 or both, to make the sound flow more smoothly.

When cutting from one shot to another it may mean cutting from one location to another location, or to an interview or a stand-up. All of these could be shot at different places where the sound conditions vary widely, such as from a busy city intersection to a quiet residential street, then to an interview shot in a quiet office. Straight cuts between these shots could be abrupt to the ear. They can be made almost seamless by simply adding **audio transitions** or **audio fades** (these names vary in different types of editing software) on the **audio timeline** between the shots. This will blend the audio from one shot to the next and be much more pleasing to the ear. Adding a simple **Dissolve** between audio cuts will achieve the same thing.

Note: Transitions tend to be set to a default length of 30 frames, or one second. This is far too long. I blend the audio for no more than 4, 6 or 8 frames. In the case of a 4 frame audio transition, that means 2 frames on either side of the cut. It doesn't sound like much, but it's all you need and makes a remarkable difference.

Don't Deliberate Too Long When Editing

If you're starting to lay in your B-roll and it's still an hour before deadline, don't relax and take advantage of that hour to leisurely finish your package. Get it cut and turn it in. News can break at any minute and you could be needed to rush to a scene and front a live shot for the top of the news or to break into programming. If you don't have your story finished, it could be someone else being sent out on that story and doing that memorable live shot that could have been great on your resume reel and that would have opened the door to your next station.

FINAL THOUGHTS

Live shot in the Sierra Nevada Mountains with former KCRA reporter Ken Pritchett, now with KTVU-TV in Oakland, California. Photo by KCRA photographer Jorge Velasquez.

Personal Views & Observations

THESE ARE A FEW PARTING THOUGHTS. Most of it's basic, common sense advice on how to do the job day in and day out. Some other parts are a little more sobering and come under the heading of "life-knowledge" that you can only acquire from having lived it. For anyone curious about entering our ranks, I feel it's important to have a clear picture of what life in this business demands of you. I don't know whether knowing any of it before would have pointed me down a different career path, but people should know what they're getting into. I'm incredibly grateful to have been a member of this profession. I'll also be the first person to speak up and say that it's not for everybody.

Ratings

Every morning TV news producers and managers scour the "overnights" (overnight ratings) analyzing the rise and drop in the number of people at home watching throughout a newscast, trying to gauge what stories people responded to and what turned them off.

I have no idea how ratings work or what a "market share" is. I don't "stack a show," meaning the order of the stories in a newscast from the lead story all the way through to the closing   copyright. I'm just a cog in the machine.

Having started out at a number three station in Kansas that few people would work for, and worked for over twenty years at a powerhouse number one station, I can tell you that it's a lot better to be at a number one than a number three. "Do ratings matter?" Yes. Ratings are absolutely what TV is all about.

Is there anything I can do to influence the numbers? I can only do my job the best I can.

Personally speaking, when I'm out on the street and someone mentions a news story they saw and it's one that I did, that makes my day. That's what ratings are to me, somebody seeing what I do and appreciating it.

Be A Good Employee—And Keep Your Job

The most winning characteristic that you can bring to the workplace is the same one that can make you a success in life—attitude. Being able to keep positive and upbeat. As I detailed about how I got my first job, it wasn't my experience that got me into this business, because I didn't have any. It was my attitude and determination. I was always willing to go out and try something or go down trying. It made me a stronger person and earned the respect of others.

When I'm sent out to shoot a simple VO-SOT where only one bite is needed, I'll try to shoot two or three extra, as well as some additional footage so that the story could be turned into a package, either by me or by an anchor or a reporter whose stories weren't panning out. It can help to fill out a newscast. It might help to give a little more exposure to the people and the story that I was sent out to cover in the first place.

When I was starting out in the business I had no idea what I was doing. During my most uncertain times at my first job in Wichita, chief photographer Jim Anderson would just give me a confident smile and say, "You're going to be okay." His belief in me helped me to believe in myself. If you can learn to be confident in yourself, then others will believe in you.

This doesn't mean saying you can do something when you can't. If you know you can't do something, be honest about it. People respect honesty. But by jumping in and giving it a try, you'll be building up your experiences and fortifying your abilities. Then, after you've been doing this for a few months or a year and you see other new people coming in on their first job looking as lost and confused as you felt at the beginning, you can look at them, put a comforting hand on their shoulder, and say, "Don't worry, you're going to get through this."

Be A Self-Starter

Don't wait for the assignment desk and the producers to come up with all your stories for you. And don't rely on the local newspapers. Find your own stories. You may get overridden by the headline of the day, but always keep your ears open. Try to get at least one story a week that you came up with on your own.

Be Honest

Always tell the truth. If you make a mistake, be the first to own up to it, take responsibility and apologize. You'll find that managers will be quicker to forgive and move on. As long as you tell the truth, you'll never have anything to hide.

A Sense of Humor

I've found few things to be truer in life than Rudyard Kipling's lines, "If you can keep your wits about you while all others are losing theirs. . . ." TV news is fraught with deadlines, tension and anxiety. If you can keep a sense of humor in a tight situation, it can go a long way towards keeping those around you relaxed.

Many times I've been standing by on a live shot during breaking news situations and heard a frantic producer talk to me over the headset, "We're not sure what's going on with this, guys. Just hold on—we should be coming to you in about five minutes."

"Five minutes? I've got time to run to McDonald's."

Carry A TV News Camera—You Carry Responsibility

When you go around with a TV camera on your shoulder you'll find that you don't have to go looking for trouble, trouble can find you. Some people will be happy to see you, some won't. Sometimes being a "member of the media" at certain events automatically marks you as "the enemy."

Always keep in mind that you represent a TV station. You have to learn to develop a thick skin and let things roll off of you. No matter what you say in defense it won't matter. A closed lip smile and a nod is often best in some situations.

This doesn't mean you should ignore a bad situation. But part of working in a job that's in the public eye is that you may receive some abuse. It isn't directed at you personally, it's just because you're with the news.

Usually when people are being loud and obnoxious to you, they're trying to incite you to get loud and angry back. If you're able to remain professional and keep a calm, low-key demeanor, it can sometimes help to diffuse an awkward situation.

Just saying, "Hey, man, I'm just here to take some pictures."

"Well, I don't want my picture taken."

"No problem. Just be turned away from me and don't look around to face the camera."

Of course, sometimes a person can be belligerent and not want you to be there. If it's a public place like a park, a street or a sidewalk, you have just as much right to be there as everybody else and shoot whatever you can see.

One crucial thing that I always do when someone comes up and starts acting confrontational is to start the camera rolling. I won't be looking through the viewfinder, but I do this to record everything that's said to me and everything that I say back. If a phone call of complaint is ever made to the station, I can protect myself with the tape. This happens rarely, but it can happen.

The Assignment Desk—You Help Them, They Help You

The people on the assignment desk go through the press releases, answer the phones and fill out the daily assignment board with who's doing what. They know what's going on. Make them your best friends.

If there's a story you want to do, pitch it to the assignment desk first. When there are twenty stories to cover and only seven shooters available, they figure out how much can get done and who can handle what. When someone calls in sick, they juggle even more. They also have the unpleasant job of having to tap someone to stay late or come in early or work a double.

I make it a policy to help the desk out as much as I can. Then when there's a story that I want to do, or a day when I need to get off a little early, they help me out.

You take care of them, they take care of you.

TV News Facts of Life

In journalism is about telling stories that are true. In life there are victories, and just as often there are defeats, compromises, and times when it's best to just walk away.

Being told, "You've got the job," was one of the greatest moments in my life. In that instant my life was changed forever. In many ways, taking a job in TV news is like taking a marriage vow because of the demands the job makes on your life.

It also comes with some hard truths. You won't find these in any text books. Some of this may not be politically correct, but it's what I've seen— and still see.

Paying Your Dues With Low-Paying Jobs

The vast majority of newsroom interns are female with dreams of being reporters and anchors with high salaries.

This is a typical scene: a young female intern will be riding along on a story and pumping the female reporter for info about what makeup looks best on TV. Occasionally, I'll pipe in:

"You shouldn't be so much concerned about your makeup as you should be about how little you're willing to work for."

"What do you mean?"

"Has anyone told you what you can expect to make at your first TV job? Maybe $15,000 a year—if you're lucky. Maybe only $13,000."

At which point the reporter may add, "I only made $13,500 at my first job. I had to share an apartment with two other girls."

After that, the intern is usually not as concerned about about makeup anymore.

You May Never Get Home Again

Many of the female interns I've talked to over the years have their future already mapped out, involving long-term boyfriends, who are invariably business majors, and plans for marriage and family within a couple of years. Sometimes I'll say to them, "You do know that if you're able to get a job as a reporter you're going to have to go away for that?"

"Oh yeah, my boyfriend and I have talked about that."

"So he's willing to move for you?"

"No, the plan is for him to get a good job here and then I'll come back in a few years."

I wish them luck. And sometimes that works out. But the plain truth is that unless you grow up in a small market town that has its own TV station, you'll probably get your first job somewhere far from home. If you're growing up in a medium to large-size city you have to be aware that as long as you work in TV news there is no guarantee that you are ever going to get home again. Once you start working in TV news the only way you may ever be able to get back home again may be if you're willing to quit TV and go into another type of profession.

I'm from St. Louis and for the first couple years that I was working in Kansas I ached to get back home. It never happened. Instead, I migrated 1,800 miles west to a station in California. This is home now.

> This is not the job for the person who wants to stay close to home and live there for thirty years right off the bat. I think I knew from the time I was a child that one day I would have to start a whole new life in a new place. And that's what I needed to do. I had to push myself, and each time you start over in a new job it gets a little easier. I don't know where I'll go next, but I am loving the journey.
>
> That's the fine reality of it. If you're a person who grows up in a beautiful city and you expect to be an anchor with flexible hours that will work around your family life, that's going to be pretty hard if not impossible to come by.
>
> "When you're a new college grad and you're looking around as a job-seeker, if you're going to limit yourself by location or salary or job title, you're going to miss out on a lot. You may be offered a larger market at a station that's not going to teach you or prepare you very well, or it could be in a very small market at a great station that has a great philosophy behind how they do the news. You have to look at what you're getting into—from a corporate level, to what the job description will be, to how that station handles breaking news and enterprise stories. There are so many things to look at and consider.
>
> I've been dating a guy for five years and more than half of that has been long distance. It's definitely been hard. There are moments when you're thinking, "What have I done? What have I done? I've moved and left everybody I've loved? What am I thinking?" But at the same time, you find a way to cope and it's hard to imagine life any other way. I think that at some point we'll be able to live in the same city. I hope that's sooner rather than later. It causes a tremendous amount of stress realizing that you're going to have to leave the person that you care about for the job you love. If you leave those you love for what you love to do, the best coping mechanism is to throw yourself into the work with everything you've got and make it count.
>
> ASHLEIGH WALTERS, WPTV-TV, West Palm Beach, Florida

TV News—A Relationship Killer

This business is brutal on private lives. Working nights, weekends and holidays—it weeds people out. Many relationships don't make it.

If you're already married when you get into news, good luck. You've got lots of bumps in the road ahead for you. My first marriage didn't make it. The long shifts, missed holidays and dedication to work didn't help—except to pay the bills.

It's better if you're already in the business before you get involved. This way the other person can see the demanding schedule and long hours you keep and what they're getting into.

I'm happy to report that I've since remarried to a great woman named Bonnie and life has never been better. It's also helped that Bonnie's only known me as a TV news photographer, so the hours and professional demands have come with the package and never been an issue.

First Job Facts of Life

The first job is typically in a small market, far from family and friends. Everybody's in the same boat—young, usually single, ambitious and working their tails off to create good reels and get better jobs. There's lots of partying and afterhours meet-ups with news people from other stations at local watering holes.

Being far from home, it's easy to get lonely. You have to be aware of what can happen when getting involved with someone "local." Invariably, that person will have lived their whole life in that town. All their family lives there—parents, brothers, sisters, aunts, uncles, cousins—and that person is never going to leave. Either you prepare to get your heart broken or forget about those larger market dreams and settle in.

Furthermore, if you're a woman in the business and want to have children, this job makes life vastly more complicated. Imagine being on-the-job and pregnant when a fire breaks out at a chemical plant. You could be the only reporter available to cover it. And news has to be covered. Something you need to consider.

The Five Year Wall

This is not an industry term but is something I've observed.

The routine career scenario is to start at an entry-level station, work there for twelve months, eighteen months, or two years. Build up the skills and a demo reel, while always keeping the eyes and ears open for the next step up the ladder. Then move up to a medium or larger market, sign a multiple-year contract, continue building up the name and reputation, maybe get an agent, and keep moving onward and upward into a top-20 market or better.

Unfortunately, not everybody makes it. Maybe it's the talent, the looks, the writing, the voice. It was good enough to get in the entry-level door, but that's as far as it goes.

Then there's the situation of a reporter who *has* got the talent and *has* got the goods, but maybe not the looks. Looks matter in TV.

A reporter may get to a medium-level station, though not exactly the station or part of the country they want, having set their sights on getting back to their hometown or some other specific city. For whatever reason that doesn't happen.

I've noticed that this seems to happen after being in the business for about five years.

A decision has to be made. Either stick it out, make the best of where you are and be the best reporter you can be—or decide that TV news isn't working for you, get out and move on to another career. TV news is an excellent training ground for P.I.O.s (Public Information Officer) and spokespersons for government agencies and public relations firms.

A third scenario is to stay on in the business, and even move up into a larger market—though not as a reporter. Many reporters make successful transitions into being producers and working the assignment desk. They're not in the limelight, but these can be stepping stones into good-paying management positions.

Aging In The Digital Age

Longevity in broadcast journalism is not something you can count on. Age is a factor in TV news. This is true both in front of and behind the camera.

Within the industry there is an oft-repeated phrase, "Younger, eager, cheaper." Outside of the networks, you see few women on-air, either as anchors or reporters, who are fifty or over. In fact, there are few women past the age of fifty in TV newsrooms at all.

Men can hold out longer, even remain on-air into their AARP years, co-anchoring a newscast with a female anchor young enough to be a daughter or granddaughter. But it doesn't work the other way around. Not fair? True. But that's TV.

Another hard truth is that once you hit your forties, whether you're male or female, the station where you're at will most likely be the station where you stay. Once you hit that ceiling you may have to stick it out. Adjust to new challenges. Roll with it. Or start looking elsewhere. And always have an "elsewhere" in the back of your mind.

In Conclusion

I love cameras. Let me repeat: *I love cameras.* I love taking pictures and having people see them. For three decades now I've been lucky enough to be paid to do that. It's not always easy, and sometimes seems almost impossible. But working together as a team, we almost always manage to make it work—some times better than others.

For as long as I've been doing this, I can still remember how long it took me to get into this business. All the odds were against me. Many times I didn't think it would happen. I've come to believe that timing is everything—if luck cracks a door open, go for it. I did.

Having worked for a couple years as a programming film editor where I spent my days isolated in a windowless editing room, I'm always grateful to have a job that gets me outside to experience a bit of what the day was like. Whether it's miserably hot or miserably cold or miserably dusty or miserably wet, at least I get to experience them.

I also like seeing places where I live. With this job, I get to see some really cool places, as well as other places that make me grateful for what I have. I've met Nobel laureates, movie stars, governors and first degree murderers. I've been given a front row seat to see what the world is like and take pictures of it, and have the privilege of having these pictures shown on TV.

One final word about this business—above all, it's a job. Thinking about the opportunity that I've been given, I can hardly to wait to go back to work in the morning, loading my gear up and ready to go.

Acknowledgments

There are many people to acknowledge for their assistance, participation and cooperation in the creation of this book.

At the top of the list, this book wouldn't exist if it hadn't been for my wife Bonnie. We were having coffee and reading the paper on New Year's morning, 2011, and we were discussing ideas for the coming year. My first book, *Naked Filmmaking*, had been out for nine months and was just starting to find its audience. Then Bonnie said, "I think you should write another book."

"*Another* book? About what?"

"About what you do—about TV news and how you do it. People are interested in TV."

So all thanks—or blame—for this book goes to Bonnie.

Next, I have to extend sincere thanks to KCRA news director Anzio Williams. The very day after Bonnie put the idea in my head, I approached him about the book. I couldn't see any way of doing this without writing about what I do at KCRA, which has been a major part of my life for the last two decades. Anzio is a strong believer in education and giving people chances to follow their dreams, and, right from the start, he fully embraced the project. His encouragement, support and participation in being interviewed, have been tremendously appreciated.

Gratitude is also extended to the employees of KCRA, both now and in the past, for making it the landmark station that it is. I learned on my very first day in the mailroom of KTVI-TV in St. Louis, Missouri, that a TV station is made up of many departments, that each has a purpose and that we all must work together to make the whole station work. I thank everyone at 3 Television Circle for the work they do and for always being willing to help me do my work.

My career was forged at KWCH-TV in Wichita, Kansas. I only wish the late Steve Ramsey was still with us. Working on this book put me back in touch with Jim Anderson, the chief photographer at KWCH-TV who molded me into a professional. I hear his critiques and words of wisdom every time I balance a camera on my shoulder.

In searching through the websites of the Wichita stations, I was happily surprised to see that a reporter I used to work with, Dave Grant, had become the news director across town at KAKE-TV. Dave put me in touch with KAKE reporter-photographer Chris Frank, who's been working the one-man way since news was shot on spring-wound 16mm film cameras and is still out there every day in the new digital environment. The photos of Chris Frank, KAKE, at work in the field are courtesy of Michael Tittinger (mikeywalks.com).

Sincere thanks to all the professionals who allowed themselves to be interviewed about their careers. Some of the people I know, such as Tracy Bryan, who I worked with for several years at KCRA before she went on to "civilian life" outside of the business; Lilian Kim, reporter at KGO-TV in San Francisco, who I also worked with and is one of my favorite people on the planet; reporter Richard Sharp, who I still see every day at KCRA and don't get to work with enough; Julie Becker-Owens, one of the first reporters I worked with at KWCH-TV, who barely tolerated me at the beginning, yet went on to become one of my lifelong best friends.

KCRA reporter Sharokina Shams put me in touch with KOBI-TV news director Julie Akins, in Medford, Oregon. Julie had been news director at KSEE-TV in Fresno and given Sharokina her break into the business. Julie unhesitatingly agreed to be part of the project.

Sharokina also suggested I talk to Wayne Freedman at KGO-TV in San Francisco. Sharokina had been at the Emmy Awards banquet when Wayne received his 50th and 51st Emmys—the 50th had been for his work as an MMJ and the 52nd was for excellence in TV news writing. Wayne, notably, is also the author of *It Takes More Than Good Looks to Succeed at Television News Reporting, 2nd Edition*, which is used in numerous universities across the country.

Wayne, in turn, recommended Ashleigh Walters (ashleighwalters.com), MMJ then at WLTX-TV in Columbia, South Carolina, and now at WPTV-TV in West Palm Beach, Florida. He also directed me to Jobin Panicker at KSEE-TV in Fresno, California.

Jacqueline Tualla (tualla.com) came recommended by several people in the KCRA newsroom as being a model example of how a student intern should work to become a professional journalist. Jacqueline was incredibly open in telling her story to me and sending pictures for the book. Jacqueline first started her career to KCOY-TV in Santa Maria, California, and is now at KOIN-TV in Salinas, California.

Thanks also to the KCRA news interns photographed for this book: Ashley Gordon, San Joaquin Delta College, Stockton; Britney Sweis, American River College, Sacramento; Amanda Clark, California State University, Sacramento; Rachel Behrmann (rachelbehr.com); Alexandria Backus, CSU Stanislaus, Turlock.

Mark Lewis (markblewis.net) shadowed me on a story during his first internship, picked my brain about the business, then immediately registered his name and started his own website.

Nha Nguyen (wix.com/nhathanhnguyen/nhatnanhnguyen), another KCRA intern success story, who went directly on to working as a reporter for KEZI-TV, Eugene, Oregon.

Naomi Lee (naomi-lee.com) first came to KCRA as an intern and has steadily been working that into a job within the newsroom, getting her foot in the broadcasting door.

The photo on the title page was taken by Nancy Siegler (nancysieglerphotography.com).

Thanks to athlete Chelsea Rodgers for the track & field sequences illustrating in & out of frame shooting. Chelsea is the daughter of KCRA sports anchor Del Rodgers.

The photos illustrating shooting-in-sequences were with KCRA intern Miranda Prado, California State University, Sacramento.

Additional photos were taken by Mike Orcutt and Marcelino Navarro (KCRA news photographers), Mike Teselle (KCRA news reporter), Dave Grant (while still a reporter at KWCH-TV, Wichita, Kansas), and KCRA intern Rachel Behrmann (rachelbehr.com).

Very big thanks to Clayton Moore and to John McWade (Before & After Magazine, bamagazine.com) for their input and contributions to the final design of the front cover.

Acknowledgement also to Lesley Kirrene and Rick Johnson with the Sacramento SPCA (Society for the Prevention of Cruelty to Animals), an outstanding organization, as are all the Sacramento animal rescue and adoption organizations. If featuring the Sacramento SPCA (sspca.org) in this book encourages anyone to open their home to an animal in need, then all the better.

Finally, as my wife Bonnie was there at the beginning, she was also there at the end to review and edit every word and every page. Any complaints, please contact her. I only did this book because she told me to.

MIKECARROLLFILMS.COM

Made in the USA
Middletown, DE
13 December 2016